PLATO
ALL THAT MATTERS

PLATO

Ieuan Williams

ALL THAT MATTERS

Also available in ebook

Contents

Introduction

Plato's philosophy, particularly his inquiries into social and political justice in his great work, the *Republic*, has repelled some of his readers and has attracted others. To his modern enemies such as Bertrand Russell, Karl Popper and Richard Crossman he is a deeply conservative, authoritarian and even totalitarian thinker, hostile to democracy and liberal values; a puritan killjoy who would dictate, regulate and supervise all aspects of human life for the purpose of establishing a highly ordered society ruled by an intellectual elite in which individuals have no choice over their status and function in society. But Plato has also attracted friends who have seen him as a great champion of justice, a philosopher seriously concerned with promoting fulfilled and happy lives for individuals and with reducing inequality and eradicating all forms of corruption. For them, Plato is a radical thinker who would grant full citizenship and equality of opportunity to women, even to the point of serving in government; who may not have seen a need for slavery in a just society; who argues for the importance of virtue, wisdom and spiritual health over ephemeral pleasure, destructive excess and corrosive decadence; who reveals the great importance of education, for both individual citizens and for the quality of culture in society; and who, finally, offers a way of freeing both individuals and political states from the endless upheavals of revolution and tyranny that in his own world condemned many individuals to lives blighted by uncertainty, anxiety and misery in unjust, corrupt and badly governed states.

▲ Plato

It is not easy to judge which of these images reflects the ideas and beliefs of the real Plato. The real Plato is elusive, in large part because of his practice of writing dialogues, dramatized discussions of philosophical questions, usually led by his teacher Socrates, a stimulating, conversational style of enquiry in which Plato himself never appears to defend his own views explicitly. What is clear, I think, is that Plato matters, and seriously so, for anyone trying to understand themselves and the world in which they belong, the world which includes both the physical nature studied by science and the social, political and cultural institutions which, for good or ill, shape their lives. The great theme that runs through all of Plato's work is that in order to pursue and achieve what is best for us we must first understand what is real, true and good, this being the province and purpose of philosophy.

There are two reasons for claiming that Plato was a great philosopher, certainly the first truly great philosopher, and, some would argue, the greatest in the history of the subject. The first is that Plato really created philosophy as it is still practised today: he identified its most fundamental problems and, over the course of a very long career, made great efforts to bring together the solutions he offered (sometimes rather tentatively) to these problems to form a comprehensive, coherent and convincing view of the world. By pursuing philosophy in his own distinctive style, by clearly formulating philosophical questions and developing the methods by which they are to be studied, Plato defined the very nature of the discipline: the whole history of philosophy is in many vitally important respects Plato's legacy.

However, there is a second reason why we must recognize the enduring value of Plato's work. His ideas and theories continue to be of enormous value for both understanding and evaluating our contemporary world, the knowledge we have acquired of it, and the current condition of our society and culture. In order to understand what matters in Plato's work it is important to bear in mind that although his philosophy has been interpreted in a variety of ways, it is now clear that Plato was not the dogmatic thinker he was generally considered to be during the centuries since he lived, but rather a philosopher who presented his thought as provocative and challenging suggestions rather than absolutely true and unquestionably claims – it is as if Plato's 'voice' is constantly saying 'this is an idea or theory that may be right; show me that it is wrong; show me that your own views are right.' When reading his dialogues it is immensely valuable to think of ourselves as engaging in a discussion with Plato rather than as simply accepting the views that are being discussed at face value. The questions and ideas discussed in his dialogues are as important to us in relation to our own society as they were to Plato in relation to the Athenian state and the moral and political improvement to which his work was ultimately directed. Plato matters, but not just to philosophers because of his influence on their subject; in spite of many differences between his Greek world and ours, Plato matters to all of us: his work challenges our most entrenched assumptions and the fundamental ideas and practices that have come to dominate our society, the moral, cultural and political 'atmosphere' we breathe without (as Plato might say) knowing whether what we absorb is good or bad for our health. The questions Plato asked are as important today as they have ever been.

Plato then and now

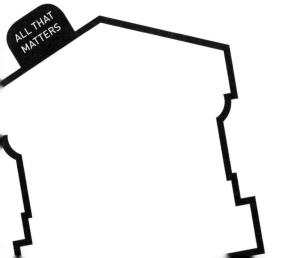

We will now look at two 'scenes', one actual and the other imaginary, which reveal much about Plato's life and philosophical mentality. The first scene that we will reconstruct, mainly from Plato's own writings, is the trial of Socrates by the Athenian court in 399 BCE, an event which clearly shows the influence of Socrates on Plato and the reasons why he became a philosopher preoccupied with ideas such as knowledge, virtue and justice. The second is Plato's imagined reaction to the financial crises which began in 2008 and from which, in 2013, Britain, together with much of the world, has still not fully recovered: from what he wrote about morality, politics and economic matters such as wealth and property, particularly in his most famous book, the *Republic*, we may be certain that Plato would have strong views on the nature and causes of this crisis.

▶ The trial of Socrates

It is 399 BCE. Five hundred citizens of the ancient Greek city of Athens, all of them men above the age of 18, are gathered in what looks like a terraced theatre. What is about to begin is the trial of a particular person and, although nobody there could have been aware of this at the time, it is a trial that is to become famous, mainly through the writings of Plato. The person on trial is probably the most well-known citizen of Athens at this time. His name is Socrates and, in the language of today's culture, he would be called a celebrity, not the kind of celebrity whose public and private life is regularly exposed in newspapers and on television, but a celebrity critic widely known for

▲ Socrates

his great intelligence, his uncompromising intellectual and personal integrity, and his fierce courage in a society which he regards as unjust and morally inadequate. Now 70 years of age, he has spent the last 30 years of his life as a public figure engaged in discussion with anyone who is prepared to meet his inquiries into the ideas and beliefs they take to be true, most often, as Socrates shows, without adequate justification.

Socrates is well known for his method of inquiry, which is really a form of interrogation. Athens is a city of conversation; the people enjoy argument and debate, and the greater part of a person's life is lived in the public arena in which Socrates plays a prominent role. If an idea such as courage or knowledge or justice crops up in conversation with others Socrates asks for a definition that should explain what the idea means; he then questions whether the definition actually does that; if the answer is unsatisfactory he asks for another definition, which is also examined critically. Even if it often happens that the discussions Plato reports in his early works do not end with a satisfactory definition, something valuable has been achieved: the confusion and falsity in the ideas discussed have been exposed, and for Socrates it is far better to give up ideas that are confused or false than to hold on to them; such ideas can be damaging, both to the person who holds them and to the community. In exposing such ideas as confused and inadequate, Socrates believes that he is acting for the benefit of individual persons and their community. However, through playing this public role Socrates has acquired a reputation, both as a critic of the moral and political ethos of the Athenian democracy and for acquiring a following, a group of young men who are strongly influenced by his activities and his character. As he will state in the trial to come, he is not surprised that charges have been brought against him: the democracy was interrupted by an oligarchy known as the 'rule of the four hundred' in 411–410 BCE, and although the democracy has been restored it remains insecure and sensitive to the kind of free critical questioning practised by Socrates and his followers.

▲ The Pynx, Athens

Plato, the most brilliant of Socrates' followers, is present at the trial and he is alarmed. The charges that Socrates has to face are serious, as Socrates himself knows. The two charges brought against him by three Athenian citizens are: 'refusing to recognize the gods of the state and introducing new gods' and 'corrupting the youth'. The Greek culture of this time recognizes many gods, but in Athens the gods of the city are officially sanctioned and the people are expected to honour them through various kinds of sacrifice and ritual. To introduce new gods would count as an act of defiance and disobedience against a city in which, as a democracy, the citizen body as a whole holds supreme authority: if Socrates is guilty of introducing new gods for himself – and he did speak of being inspired by supernatural voices – then he is clearly guilty of defying the authority of the city itself. By modern standards the population of Athens is very small indeed, larger than other Greek states but still, at its maximum, a population of only around 5,000 adult male citizens, all of them eligible to participate in a democracy. In short, the body of Athenian citizens, which excludes women, slaves and foreign workers (of whom there were a considerable number) is rather a closed community, more like a large club governing its own membership and conduct than the kind of modern democracy with which we are familiar. For an individual to offend against this body of men is so grave that if Socrates is found guilty there is a sense in which he will have failed to live up to his own status as a citizen and will be punished accordingly.

The second charge against Socrates is also politically significant but more difficult to understand. It has much to do with the way of life he has been following within the Athenian city. He has been in many ways an exemplary citizen: he has obeyed the laws of the city, fought courageously as a soldier in war, and served for a period as a conscientious member of the Athenian Council. And yet, through his open criticism of Athenian society, together with his influence on his young admirers, Socrates is now seen by many as a threatening figure: questioning the values of those in authority and publicly reminding them of the standards they fail to meet, then as now, is not likely to make one popular, and for many in the Athenian democracy Socrates has become an irritating voice, a man to be silenced, not to be heard with respect. If the charge of corrupting the minds of the young men means anything in the Athenian city, it is that Socrates is believed to have turned his followers, some of them conservatives from aristocratic families, against democratic government.

The trial begins with the accusers presenting the charges that Socrates will have to face. Then Socrates speaks at length in his own defence, boldly declaring that scarcely a word that has been said is true and that he will not resort to the kind of flowery language used by his accusers. This is the voice of Socrates as Plato reported it:

> 'My accusers have said little or nothing that is true, but from me you shall hear the whole truth; not, I can assure you, gentlemen, in flowery

language like theirs, decked out with fine words and phrases; no, what you will hear will be a straightforward speech in the first words that occur to me, confident that as I am in the justice of my cause.'

(Defence of Socrates 17a–c)

Contrary to rumours that have been circulating, he is not an atheist, and he insists that those who have heard him in discussion and argument in the city will know that his only interest is in the truth and the wisdom that only truth and knowledge can bring about. In fact, as he points out, the wisdom he has gained is of a distinctive kind. A friend had asked the Oracle at Delphi whether Socrates was the wisest man in the world and the Oracle had agreed that he was. After thinking hard about this Socrates had come to the conclusion that all his wisdom actually amounted to was a very simple principle: 'that I do not think that I know what I do not know'. However, many of his fellow Athenians do not seem to accept that principle, and Socrates acknowledges that his practice of habitually questioning their beliefs and exposing their lack of knowledge and understanding has aroused considerable hostility towards him. But his reputation for corrupting the young by filling their heads with false ideas is totally false: his intention has never been to persuade people to accept his own ideas and beliefs but to lead them to reflect critically on the ideas and beliefs they already have. This may seem a negative practice, but to be liberated from confusion and ignorance – the main purpose of philosophy – is vitally important, both for the individual citizen and for the community.

The speech continues. Socrates concedes that the hostility towards him may well bring about his destruction, but he refuses to compromise and express any regret in order to secure an acquittal. He has no fear of death and insists that his way of life has been that of a good citizen whose pursuit of truth and wisdom on behalf of his fellow Athenians has been of great benefit to the city. If the jury did offer to acquit him on condition that he would give up his public role he would refuse to do so. He states that he has a higher duty towards God than to his fellow Athenians, and for as long as he lives he will go on practising philosophy in the public life of the city. He will continue to say to anyone who will listen:

'My friend, you are an Athenian and belong to a city which is the greatest and most famous in the world for its wisdom and strength. Are you not ashamed that you give your attention to acquiring as much money as

possible, and similarly with reputation and honour, and give no attention or thought to truth and understanding and perfection of your soul?'

(Defence of Socrates 29d–e)

This response is of great interest and perhaps reveals both why Socrates has lived as he has done and why he is so admired by Plato. He is motivated by concern for the highest welfare of the souls of his fellow citizens, which implies that the moral character of the community depends on the virtuous souls and lives of individuals: what brings about injustice in the city is as much a matter of individual immorality as it is of political policies that favour those who are rich and powerful. As the reference to the pursuit of wealth indicates, both Socrates and Plato were concerned about the damaging effects that could result from the unrestrained desire for money and power, and we will take this up in the next section.

The trial is nearing its end. Socrates' speech is not persuasive and he is found guilty of both charges. However, the number of votes cast for a guilty verdict is not sufficient to carry the death penalty and, according to legal practice, Socrates is allowed to propose an alternative punishment. Socrates is poor and suggests a fine that will be low enough to enable him to pay it. This is not accepted by the court and the death penalty is imposed. These are Socrates' last words to the court:

> '*Now it is time that we were going, I to die and you to live; but which of us has the happier prospect is unknown to anyone but God.*'

(*Defence of Socrates 42a*)

Socrates' response to the verdict passed on him by the court makes a great impression on Plato. It was perfectly possible for Socrates to have escaped and gone into exile but he did not. As an individual who takes his status as an Athenian citizen seriously, he believes it necessary to live by the city's laws and to abide by the verdict passed on him, even though he believes it to be wrong.

As a result of Socrates' execution, Plato becomes disillusioned with politics and gives up the idea of following a political career, concluding that it was almost impossible 'to take part in public life and retain one's integrity'. Socrates' example inspires Plato to take up philosophy, although not in the style of his teacher. His concerns are more positive than those of Socrates and in the course of a long career Plato builds up an impressive body of writings in which he investigates fundamental questions about the nature of the world, human beings, knowledge, communication, morality, political justice and art. But the example set by Socrates never leaves him; he represents for Plato the very spirit of philosophy, the integrity the discipline demands, the depth of understanding it pursues, and the vital contribution critical reflection can make to our understanding ourselves and our actions. His execution also fosters in Plato a deep suspicion of Athenian democracy, which he regards as unjust. His response to democracy, as well as to other forms of unjust political systems, is to be found in his most famous work, the *Republic*, which we will discuss in later chapters. It is, however, useful to mention here that Plato believed that Athenian democracy encouraged a number of human desires which led to injustice and unhappiness, one of those being a strong desire – perhaps we would now use the word obsession – for wealth and personal advantage. We will now consider what Plato's attitude might have been to the same kind of desire in contemporary capitalist societies.

▶ Plato and the banking crisis

Great philosophers have distinctive 'voices' that continue to speak to us in the contemporary world. The problems they were concerned with, and the manner in which they tackled them, were, of course, very much of their own time and circumstances. But those problems have tended to recur quite regularly in human history with the same seriousness and urgency, particularly during periods of crisis and decline.

Although the problems that concern us today are not the same in every detail as those that worried Plato, the ideas and theories that are at the heart of Plato's philosophy still challenge our most fundamental assumptions in such

▲ Margaret Thatcher and Ronald Reagan

areas of interest as scientific inquiry, human psychology, morality, politics, economics, education and art. We will now illustrate how valuable Plato's philosophy can be for understanding and evaluating important features of contemporary society by imagining what would have been his likely response to the economic crisis which began in 2008, taking as our clue Socrates' comment, near the end of his defending speech, about the pursuit of wealth. Plato shared Socrates' anxiety over the excessive pursuit of wealth and its consequences for both individuals and the moral culture of society. The key idea for understanding this issue is Plato's idea of the human soul, one of his most important contributions to philosophy and our topic in chapter five.

In Plato's view, the soul was the reality of a person; it constituted a person's identity and everything that was essential to being a human being rather than a member of another species. What is interesting in connection with Plato's anxiety over money-making, particularly the aim of accumulating as much money as possible for its own sake, is the fact that his idea of the soul, as well as including our capacity to reason (and thus the ability to acquire knowledge) also included what we would now call moral character, the kind of person someone is in terms of moral virtue and goodness. Since money-making is, for Plato, closer to being an obsession than a productive and valuable practice, it must necessarily have a damaging effect on the moral state of a person's soul. Indeed, Plato believed that the unrestrained pursuit of financial gain had already damaged both the Athenian city and the lives of its citizens. The political system by which Athens was governed during most of Plato's life was democracy, a system which, Plato believed, encouraged the desire for luxury and (just as in an oligarchic state actually governed by the wealthy) the pursuit of personal wealth and advantage. At the height of her power Athens had been the economic centre both of her own large empire and the wider Greek world that extended around the Mediterranean. Money, in the form of metal coinage, had become supremely important as the medium through which the Greek economy functioned and this, in Plato's view, had profoundly affected the character of Athenian life. His observations form a long list: the possession of wealth had become the primary source of status and power; it had become the cause of serious inequality, dissatisfaction and conflict within the city;

it distracted individuals from living virtuously; it had contributed significantly to military defeat by Sparta in the Peloponnesian War and a drastic loss of prestige and power.

Perhaps we are now beginning to form an idea of what Plato's response to the economic character of our own society might have been. At the heart of the financial crisis that began in 2008 was the banking system and Plato was certainly familiar with banking and the problems it could cause in the Greek world of his time. Manufacturers, merchants and retail traders deposited money in banks, banks facilitated financial exchanges, and banks gave credit, sometimes on a very large scale: the richest banker in Athens during Plato's life, a man called Pasion, was reputed to have at one time as much as 300,000 drachmas on loan, the equivalent of many millions in pounds or dollars. Banks and bankers not only became enormously rich and powerful, they were also, as in our own time, prone, through malpractice and incompetence, to the kind of failure and its consequences with which we are very familiar. Banking practices in Athens and the Greek world did come to be legally regulated but not, in Plato's view, as extensively and rigorously as they ought to have been. Plato would have been fascinated by the parallels between his economic world and ours.

It is now widely agreed that the most fundamental cause of the economic catastrophe of 2008 was the deregulation of the financial industries, which for some time had included the largest banks. The function of regulation, in fields as diverse as traffic control and the monitoring of animal experimentation, is to constrain, and always for reasons: the avoidance of chaos on our roads and in our cities; the prevention of excessive pain and distress to animals. In the financial world the function of regulation is, quite clearly, to ensure fairness and responsibility in a competitive field of practice that would otherwise be prone to manipulation for unfair advantage and dangerously irresponsible conduct. But the deregulation that began in the early 1980s was not

▲ Greek coins

introduced for its own sake; it was essentially tied to an economic theory (or, less kindly, an ideology) according to which, (i) regulation constitutes a form of intervention in economic and financial markets, and (ii) markets worked best for the creation of profit, wealth, and general prosperity when they are least interfered with, a theory defended by F. A. von Hayek and Milton Friedman, two of the most influential economists of the time.

However, the consequences of deregulating the financial industry do not seem to be what was anticipated: just as the abolition of traffic regulations results in chaos, so the consequences of deregulation, introduced when Margaret Thatcher was Prime Minister of Britain and Ronald Reagan

▲ FA von Hayek

President of the United States, led to the proliferation of exceptionally complex and risky practices that would eventually bring chaos to national economies, and indeed to the global economy, and the failure of some of the largest banks and investment companies. The selling of sub-prime mortgages was but one example of such practices. In the United States banks that had entered the field of mortgages granted loans to very large numbers of house buyers who were, in the long term, unlikely to be able to repay the sums they had borrowed. This extremely risky practice – one wonders whether it could it be described as rational let alone as ethically acceptable – was highly profitable in the short term, but when borrowers began to default on their repayments in large numbers, which should have been entirely predictable, the lending institutions began to lose very large sums of money.

In the aftermath of this disaster it emerged that banks, which had now become investment banks with shareholders, had, in company with other financial firms and companies, devised strategies of investment and speculation which amount to little more than gambling on commodity prices, futures, fluctuations in rates of exchange within the system, and so forth. And they had done so on a massive scale, both for massive profits and for the payment of massive bonuses to those who exploited these strategies successfully. The ultimate result of such activity was debt, once again on a huge, barely imaginable, scale, and the collapse of banks and other financial bodies, not from responsible investment (although investment always carries some degree of risk) but by exploiting the economic system itself purely for the accumulation of wealth. The effect of the crisis was disastrous for large numbers of individuals and families in many societies: unemployment on a large scale, a rise in poverty, the loss of homes, and insecurity for many individuals who had to pay the price for those who were guilty of causing the catastrophe, theorists and politicians as well as those who, in practice, brought it all about.

Plato, as a great champion of regulation, would surely have challenged any belief in the advantageous consequences of deregulation, but zealots are, by definition, incapable of heeding warnings from those they invariably regard as unconverted sceptics. For Plato, their belief in unfettered markets would be wholly unwarranted, a serious failure to see that the kind of unconstrained and weakly supervised changes that can occur, both in an economy and in a society, will always lead to disaster and human harm. We are not, of course, concerned here with natural change, the motion of a falling object or an orbiting planet, for example, but change as a consequence of human actions, such as financial investment, and the processes they maintain, such as the return on investment at a rate of interest. Such processes, Plato would have argued, ought to be under intelligent and responsible control and directed at the well-being of individuals in a just society: in the absence of constraints an economic system will inevitably be exploited for profit and advantage by those with no concern for the community that will suffer the consequences of their greed. To abandon regulation in the name of an economic and political ideology, an abstract and unproven dogma, would, Plato would have claimed, inevitably have led to the very disaster that actually occurred in 2008. Plato would have advised us to think carefully about the real nature of the economic aspect of society and to give serious thought to what economic activities and practices ought to achieve: an economy is not detached from human choice, intention and action in the way that natural occurrences obviously are – the economic life of a society can and ought to be made subject to human decision and control and should be made to work for justice rather than for feeding the avarice of private individuals and institutions.

Plato's critical reflections are very much in harmony with his views on human life and society in general. Plato was a great believer in the importance of authority, and authority, unlike the force of gravity, for example, is essentially human and involves rules that both constitute and constrain forms of human thought and action. For Plato, the absence of authoritative constraints does not result in real freedom but, more often than not, in disorder, disunity and injustice.

2

Before Plato: the search for order

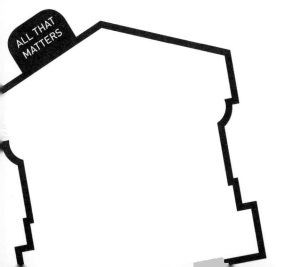

Philosophy began in the city of Miletos in the Greek province of Iona at around 600 BCE. The subject that interested the philosophers of Miletos was nature (*phusis*) and they created theories to explain how nature is ordered and, therefore, coherent; an aim which at this time philosophy shared with science. Nature is clearly not chaotic, events and processes are not random or haphazard but regular and predictable. Why? The first philosopher we know of, a man called Thales, suggested that water was the key to understanding change and order: water is in all things, it is necessary to life, and, as an agent of change, it can transform a substance, earth for example, from being in one state to being in another. The man who may have been a student of Thales at Miletos, Anaximander, proposed a different hypothesis. All things were made of the same substance which he called the *apeiron*, an indeterminate, infinite stuff from which all things came into existence and into which they returned after they had declined and perished: reality is one thing but, as experienced by human beings, it takes many different forms. It was the *apeiron* that was responsible for ordered change in the world, the law-like regularity of events and processes.

The most interesting general feature of these theories was that they were intended to explain nature, not by reference to anything external to the world, such as the gods of Greek mythology, but to substances that were clearly within nature itself. And Anaximander seems to have been committed to at least one of the fundamental principles of naturalism, both in modern as well as ancient philosophy, which is that human beings must

▲ Ancient Greece

be understood as being entirely within physical nature and, therefore, subject to the same kind of theory and explanation as everything else. Plato, as we shall see presently, was not a defender of naturalism.

The philosophers who had the greatest impact on Plato's thought came slightly later than the early Milesians. Plato was certainly influenced by Pythagoras and his followers, particular their very modern idea that nature can in some sense be understood through mathematics, but it is the work of two philosophers, Heraclitus and Parmenides, that is most important to Plato's philosophical development. Heraclitus was an immensely obscure thinker but it is possible to pick out a number of important ideas from writings: (i) everything is in a state of change but this change is ordered rather than chaotic; there is, he claimed, a *logos* (reason, intelligence, formula) in nature which gives the universe both unity and meaning; (ii) the *logos* cannot be understood through sense experience – the senses are limited and deceptive – but only through reason. But Heraclitus, although he did not think reality could be explained by reference to a material substance such as water or the *apeiron*, shared the naturalism of his Milesian predecessors, claiming that the human soul, which included the real nature of persons as well as their capacity to reason, was, like the *logos*, entirely within nature. This, as we shall see, was not a principle Plato could accept.

Parmenides was a very different philosopher, one who aimed at the greatest possible clarity and certainty. He was an influential and challenging thinker who was the first to introduce into philosophy the method of rigorous argument, the kind of thought that aims to draw undeniably true conclusions in accordance with the strict rules of logic. For Parmenides it was a method by which some of the most fundamental words in language can be subjected to the most rigorous conceptual and logical scrutiny, words such as 'is', 'is not', 'being' and 'non-being'. He was interested in the exact meanings of these terms in the context of logically sound argument, a practice that remains of crucial importance in philosophy to this day. This, in outline, is how Parmenides employed this method. We can only say something about what *is* or really exists; we cannot say anything about nothing (non-being) since there can be no such thing; therefore, what we try to say about what 'is not', will be meaningless; it follows that we can only make meaningful statements about what *is*. But this is puzzling. We can make false as well as true statements, but since false statements cannot be about anything they must be meaningless, which also seems to imply that all meaningful statements will be true. Parmenides' conclusion was wrong, of course, but he himself could not solve the paradox that his method of argument had thrown back at him. That method had also led him to some strange conclusions concerning the nature of reality. We can only make meaningful statements about what is real, but what is real (what *is*) cannot change, it must at all times be itself and nothing else; if it changes it becomes different and will no longer be exactly itself. Reality, Parmenides concluded, is quite unlike the *appearances* of the things we are familiar with in our experience: reality does not change, it is one thing rather than many different things, and, because it does not change, must be timeless.

The legacy bequeathed to Plato by Heraclitus and Parmenides is a list of problems: in the case of Heraclitus, to explain the *logos* and thus to understand how nature is ordered and unified, to clarify the real nature of the soul, and to grasp the status of human life in relation to the natural order; in the case of Parmenides, to explain how there can be false as well as true statements, to explain convincingly how words have meaning and thus to understand how knowledge and communication are possible, to show that the difference between appearance and reality can't be as radical as Parmenides' arguments made it out to be.

However, Plato was aware of an important difference between the work of Heraclitus and that of Parmenides. Heraclitus was interested in nature, in the problem, initiated by the Milesian philosophers, of explaining the order and unity of nature. With Parmenides we see a change of interest, more in the thought and language in which nature is represented, explained and understood rather than in nature as we experience it. This change was to have a profound influence on Plato's work.

3

Socrates and the Sophists: the search for authority

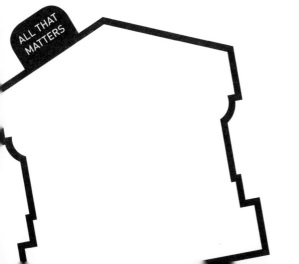

ALL THAT
MATTERS

If Socrates was the father of philosophy then Plato was the son who took further and completed his teacher's project. The crucial assumption behind that project was that philosophy is not wholly abstract and remote from the concrete circumstances of human life. Both teacher and student believed that philosophy was vitally important to understanding the world, the nature of humanity in relation to that world, and, perhaps most significantly, the task of improving the lives of individuals in a society in which they can truly flourish. We already know how Socrates carried out his work from his defence at his trial. We will now concentrate on Socrates' interest in morality and knowledge in the context of his opposition to the ideas and practices of the Sophists, an apposition that Plato continued and made a persistent theme in his writings. Who and what were the Sophists and why did they attract such disapproval? The answer is simply that they did not share the same philosophical, moral and political concerns as Socrates and Plato; their aim was to thrive in the world as it was rather than to improve it; they were pragmatists who taught the skills and techniques by which citizens could further their material and political advantage in a culture dominated by individual competitiveness and ambition, a culture in some ways resembling the culture that has come to dominate life in Britain since the early 1980s. The Sophist, like our experts in advertising, marketing and public relations, were concerned with persuasion rather than with communicating knowledge and understanding. For both Socrates and Plato the ideas and practices of the Sophists,

▲ Agora

the demand for their services and the success they achieved were all symptoms of a serious deterioration in the moral and political culture of Athens, a form of deterioration the Sophists furthered rather than worked towards arresting and reversing it.

The Sophists were itinerant teachers who came to Athens from a number of cities in the Greek world – Gorgias from Leontini in Sicily and Protagoras from the city of Abdera – and their area of expertise, broadly understood, might be called 'life management', giving advice to citizens on how to achieve success in the city. What Plato saw very clearly was that the skills of effective oratory that were taught by the Sophists could not themselves explain and communicate the authority of moral ideas and principles. By the time the Sophists arrived in Athens the lives of citizens had become increasingly individualistic, competitive and shaped by economic ambitions. The Sophists gave Athenians precisely what they wanted: the rhetorical techniques of persuasion and the philosophical ideas that were believed justify them. Socrates, on the other hand, had very different concerns and neither taught his fellow Athenians the skills they wanted nor told them what they wanted to hear. It is in connection with this difference that we may grasp the purpose of Plato's work, which was to establish an authority for moral beliefs and practices, an authority that did not rest on the foundations of religion or tradition but which was, nevertheless, compelling. The means by which that authority can be revealed was philosophical thought, a form of inquiry that could effectively oppose the trends in Athenian life that had created the very needs that the skills of the Sophists were intended to meet.

Philosophy is concerned with ideas and with the meanings of the words by which ideas are applied and communicated. Plato had realized that there was an important similarity between the aims of Parmenides' method of argument and the purpose behind Socrates' discussions with his fellow citizens. In spite of differences, both were concerned with clarifying and establishing the real meanings of words and ideas:

in Parmenides' work the words necessary for gaining knowledge of reality; in Socratic practice the words involved in understanding the nature of persons, the kind of life they ought to lead, and the kind of society in which they ought to live. Plato became convinced that if these words did not possess objective and authoritative meanings then achieving knowledge, including knowledge of what it is to pursue virtuous lives and maintaining justice in society, would be impossible. And that was precisely what the Sophists did say: words did *not* have fixed and objective meanings; meaning was conventional and flexible, determined by human interests and decisions. This weakening of the authority of meaning led the Sophists to view meaning from what, according to Plato, was the wrong perspective, one in which meaning is not understood in terms of a relationship between language and the world but rather the relationship between language and speakers who use it to further their interests in particular forms of interaction such as that between an orator and his audience. The function of language, from this perspective, is not to represent the world truthfully in accordance with the right rules and principles but to further individual advantage. For Plato this way of understanding language was seriously mistaken and pointed towards the kind of discourse that promoted injustice and unhappiness in a community rather than what was good for human beings. The Sophist's idea of language as an instrument of persuasion, rather than as a medium of genuine communication, rested on two theories that Plato believed should be strenuously resisted, scepticism and relativism.

Scepticism is the thesis that knowledge is impossible; claims to know, rather than merely to believe, are always open to doubt because they can never meet the standards of truth and certainty by which knowledge is defined. Gorgias, a prominent Sophist, clearly defended a form of scepticism. He was said to have made three claims which seem wildly contrary to common sense: nothing exists; if anything did exist we could not know it; even if we did know it we could not communicate it to anyone else. However Gorgias meant these claims to be taken – was he actually claiming that they were true? – they are related in important ways to the skills of oratory that Gorgias taught his students. Scepticism with regard to knowledge of reality, which also doubts that there can be objective meaning and unquestionable truth, had the effect of liberating language from the rules which govern the meaningful use of words and determine the possibility of saying what is true. For Plato this amounted to denying the authority of *logos*, understood, not as the order of nature referred to by Heraclitus, but as the logically ordered use of words in argument, representation and communication. This, as Plato saw it, was the problem: in the absence of the constraints of *logos* a speaker seems to be free to regard words as weapons that may be used in the verbal combat that went on in democratic politics, legal proceedings and commercial affairs.

The other doctrine that troubled Plato was relativism. We still associate relativism with Protagoras, the Sophist whom Plato most respected even though he believed his views to be seriously mistaken. Protagoras expressed the theory of relativism in a famous statement: 'Man is the measure of all things, of the things that are that they are, and of things that are not that they are not.' This has generally been taken to mean that what is true for one person or group is not necessarily true for another individual or group, which clearly implies that there are no standards of truth that are independent of the perceptions of particular individuals or the beliefs shared by members of social groups. Plato saw very clearly that the statement 'Man is the measure of all things' had the effect of shifting the standards governing what we ought to believe and say from the world to either the subjective experiences of individuals or the conventions of a particular social group: it is not the world and its impact on our experience that determines what we should believe and say about it, rather, it is the individual's experiences that are to determine what we believe and say about the world. And, once again, we can see how this change seems to imply what some might regard as a welcome liberation from the constraints imposed on experiences and thought by a world that is independent of how we happen to experience and understand it.

This is Protagoras' argument. Suppose that one person states that the wind is cold and another states that it is warm. According the principle that the subjective experience of individual persons serves as the only criterion of truth, we cannot say that one of these is right and the other wrong: it is simply not possible to 'get outside' individual experiences to establish whether the wind is either cold or hot: it is cold for one person and hot for the other. Individual experiences are notoriously variable, but they are the only 'measure', the only 'judge', of the way things are. Truth, therefore, is entirely relative to how we experience things, a principle that also applies to moral values and beliefs. The fact that different societies and cultures approve of different kinds of moral belief and practice invited the conclusion that there were no universal and unquestionable truths concerning morality and justice and that the meaning of such words as 'virtue' and 'justice' simply reflected the interests and circumstances of different social groups: what counted as virtue and justice for one group need not count as virtue and justice for another group. This was the relativism that Plato found disturbing and strove to refute. Whether he actually succeeded, and indeed whether anyone has, remains a matter of controversy.

The main argument by which Plato attacked Protagoras' claim that 'Man is the measure of all things' seems to be both straightforward and impressive. It turns on the familiar fact that human beings often disagree with each other, the fact that while some individuals may believe that a particular statement is true others may believe that it is false. In his dialogue, the *Theaetetus*, written fairly late in Plato's career, we are invited to apply this observation to Protagoras' own claim that 'Man is the measure of all things'. We must assume that in making this statement Protagoras actually believed that it was true for him. What, then, are we to say about those who believe that the statement is false, again for them? Surely they are equally entitled to believe and say that 'Man is *not* the measure of all things.' After all,

Protagoras' claim depends entirely on the assumption that there can be no statement that that is true *in itself* but only true *for* a particular individual or group. This is Plato's argument:

1 Protagoras' claim is believed to be true by Protagoras and is, therefore, true *for* him;

2 Protagoras' claim is believed to be false by others and, therefore, it is false *for* them;

3 Protagoras must accept that those who disagree with his statement believe that it is true *for* them;

4 Therefore, Protagoras must accept that his own claim, 'Man is the measure of all things', is both true and false, true *for* him and false *for* others.

Plato believed that we ought to find this conclusion disturbing: it implies that one and the same statement can be both true and false, depending entirely on the beliefs that individual persons happen to hold. By subjecting Protagoras' claim to logical scrutiny Plato was able to bring out clearly that in conceding that a statement can be both true and false (at the same time) Protagoras' theory violated the most fundamental principle of human reason, which is that all statements *must* be either true or false. The very possibility that statements may be both true and false at the same time makes reasoning impossible: all arguments depend on the statements they contain being either true or false but not both. The task of showing that there are some statements that cannot be doubted or denied, while other kinds of statement certainly can be, is taken up by Plato in his next great dialogue, the *Sophist*. What he shows in the *Theaetetus* is that Protagoras was simply unable to offer a clear account of the difference between truth and falsity, more precisely an account of what made a statement true rather than false: whatever that is, it can't be subjective experience, conventional agreement, or, something we are very familiar with in our own time, what suits the interests of those in political power.

For Plato the consequences of relativism were serious, far more so than those who, in our own time, encourage us to accept, lightly and cheerfully, the doctrine actually realize. When we call particular statements true we are, by implication, ruling out other statements as false, for unless that was the case the very ideas of truth and falsity would be completely meaningless and unusable: once the distinction between truth and falsity is made either entirely subjective or subject to human interests and agreement within a group, the very possibility of genuine discourse, of accurate representation, clear expression and real communication, is destroyed. This possibility haunts Plato's thinking about language and media. It is a matter that we should be as concerned about as Plato.

4

Language and media: the search for communication

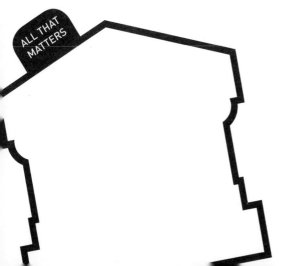

Media are hugely important: it is through language that human beings communicate and are able to live together in families, communities and societies; it is in the medium of mathematical symbolism that science ultimately comprehends the world; it is in the media of words, images and sounds that those with talent and skill create the works of art that are a part of a society's culture. Plato was the first philosopher to recognize the profound importance of media and to make the nature and significance of media one of the fundamental topics of philosophical inquiry. But what are media? What is the value of media in human life? How should media be involved in society, culture and the conduct

▲ A 1950s advert for TV

of government? These are Plato's questions and they should also be ours at the present time: media are not only a subject of interest; they are also a cause for anxiety.

The medium that dominated Athenian life in Plato's time was, of course, language; early in his career, Plato became intensely interested in the practice of oratory, the art of public speaking taught by the Sophists. But he also became interested in media in general, in the use of image and form in painting, sculpture, architecture and decoration and in the use of sound in the composition and performance of music. As always with Plato, his interest covered both the nature of media and their consequences for human life, their value in relation to human well-being in the communities in which they lived.

This was Plato's most fundamental observation: a medium consists of signs that can be arranged to bring about representation, expression and communication. This implied, first, that a medium such as language must be understood in terms of concepts such as meaning, truth and coherence (in the language of ancient Greece the word *logos*, which we have already encountered, connected the use of language with reason and order), and second, that a medium involves the possibility of expressing what is false and of deceiving and manipulating others as well as expressing what is true, honest and transparent. Plato's discussions of media in a number of his most important dialogues reveal that language and media possess three aspects, a semantic aspect concerning the meanings of words and the statements expressed by sentences, an ethical aspect concerned with the morally permissible uses of media, and a political aspect concerned with the relationship between media and justice in society. In this chapter we will concentrate on the ethical and semantic aspects and take up the political aspect in connection with justice.

▶ The ethical aspect

What troubled Plato was the simple fact that media can be used to bring about conviction in the minds of persons in the complete absence of knowledge and understanding. Because conviction is a subjective mental state a person can be completely convinced that a statement is true when it is in fact false: conviction, Plato realized, cannot guarantee that a statement is true; rather, we are only entitled to be convinced when we know that a statement is true. The ability to convince through the use of media gave great power to those who were able to use signs effectively, and power, as we know, can be abused. Plato's concerns here were, of course, bound up with his unwavering belief that the techniques of oratory taught by the Sophists were dangerous and that those techniques, because they had become woven into the fabric of Athenian politics, had done much to further the growth of injustice.

How did Plato clarify the ethical aspect of media? The Sophist Gorgias, in Plato's dialogue that bears his name, claims that oratory is a genuine art and one that confers great advantages on those who have mastered it. He also claims that oratory can teach the difference between what is right and wrong. Socrates challenges these claims. In response to the question of whether oratory, like a genuine art such as medicine, has a subject matter of its own, Gorgias is forced to concede that oratory does not actually have its own field of knowledge, or, as in medicine, the kind of internal rational structure by which a genuine art can be distinguished from its counterfeit forms.

Gorgias' second claim concerning the difference between right and wrong takes us to the heart of the ethical aspect of media. Socrates destroys this claim by appealing to the fact that oratory can be used unethically, to deceive, to arouse irrational fears, to reinforce prejudices, and to manipulate emotional reactions, all of which can be condemned as morally unacceptable. The very fact that oratory can be used in morally unacceptable ways for morally unacceptable purposes reveals very clearly that oratory cannot actually *teach* the difference between right and wrong: oratory is subject to moral standards that are independent of oratory itself; oratory, Socrates concludes, is a counterfeit form of art or discipline, similar in kind to the techniques of the beautician by which the appearance, rather than the reality, of health and beauty can be created. Through techniques of persuasion, oratory can create the appearance but not the reality of communication.

But if oratory is a counterfeit form of practice, what is the genuine art that it imitates? And how, as a bogus form of art, does it work? Plato's answers to these questions are interesting and valuable. The real art of which oratory is a counterfeit form is, broadly understood, the art of government, an art that must, whether in the form of self-government or the government of a political state, involve knowledge and understanding in order to be legitimate and genuinely educative. Oratory is an instrument of persuasion and manipulation rather than a genuinely educative art that is of genuine value, both for self-government and for legitimate authority in a political state. As to the second question, oratory works, like much of modern advertising, by flattery, not by expressing what is true but by pandering to vices such as vanity and a concern with status rather than by appealing to a person's intelligence and virtue; it is a knack, a collection of techniques that may be acquired by trial and error rather than a genuine field of knowledge. The conclusion of Plato's discussion in the *Gorgias* is that the use of language and other media must be subject to independent and authoritative ethical standards, standards he later shows are necessary not only to determine acceptable uses of signs but which make the very use of signs possible. The Sophists took the view that there were no such standards: can it be shown that they were wrong?

▶ The semantic aspect

The ideas of meaning and truth constitute the semantic aspect of language and media, but these, Plato insists, must be real rather than merely apparent if genuine communication is to be possible. In his late and important dialogue, the *Sophist,* Plato took on the task of showing that the three conditions that make meaningful discourse possible could actually be met. These conditions are: (i) that words do not change their meaning from person to person and from place to place; (ii) that there must be principles according to which words can be put together to form meaningful statements; and (iii) that there must be a real difference between truth and falsity. Plato's strategy in the dialogue appeals to what is known as the theory of Forms or ideas, one of his most important contributions to philosophy: real communication, as Plato puts it in the *Sophist*, 'owes it existence to the weaving together of Forms' (*Sophist* 259e), or, as we might now say, to the structure of our concepts.

The essence of Plato's argument is this. Many of the words that we use, and certainly the words that are most fundamental to understanding the world, ourselves and our values, derive their real or objective meanings from ideas or, as Plato calls them, Forms, ideas that are real and cannot be altered by human beings to suit their interests and purposes. Just as human beings are able to experience things through the senses, they are also able to understand ideas, a good example of this being our ability to understand numbers and thus to use them correctly in our calculations. It is by understanding ideas that we are able to know what words really mean, words such as 'animal', 'space', 'time', 'equal', 'triangle', 'four', 'soul', 'virtue', 'justice', and very many others, words that are important to us in relation to knowledge and the way we live. Because such words are linked very closely to particular ideas, the meanings of such words are not, according to Plato, created by human beings, nor do they arise from conventional practice: these days the word 'refute' is commonly used to mean the same thing as 'reject' or 'deny', which is not what Plato would call its real or objective meaning: 'refute' actually means to disprove a conclusion or to expose the flaws in an argument, but the convention now is to use it simply as an equivalent for 'reject'.

When we arrange words into coherent sentences, what they express may be true or false depending on how things are in the world: 'It is raining' is true when it is actually raining, false when it is not. The structure of ideas or Forms which underlie language guarantee that our use of words is correct and meaningful because that structure is itself coherent and contains within itself the most fundamental truths about the nature of the world, truths about the order of nature, about change and motion, space and time, the identities of things, the classification of species, the nature of the human soul and human behaviour, about virtue, justice and happiness. Ideas or Forms have what may be called 'content', which is what we know when we acquire an idea. When we come to understand the idea of time, for example, we come to understand the ideas it contains, familiar ideas such as moment, interval, before and after, past, present and future: to be able to tell the time, measure the time between events, and to use words such as 'past', 'present' and 'future' is precisely what it means to say that we understand the idea or Form of time. The 'contents' of our ideas, and thus the real meanings of the words linked to them, can be revealed by analysis and argument, a process which Plato called dialectic: it is the real meaning of the word 'justice' that is the subject of Plato's great dialogue, the *Republic*.

The theory of ideas has always been controversial. The fact that many of its critics have concentrated on the question of whether these ideas or Forms really exist has, I think, been an obstacle to fully appreciating why the theory is important to Plato's philosophy, particularly to his account of language and media. Plato was claiming that the most important words in our language have objective meanings that they derive from those objects that he called ideas or Forms. But does the truth of the theory depend on there actually being such objects? Well, such objects cannot exist in the way that physical objects exist, which is connected with the fact that ideas cannot change in the way that physical objects change, through fading colour, rusting, crumbling, and so forth; they are abstract and thus 'objects' of understanding that we can 'grasp', like the way we grasp numbers, for example, in combination with other ideas and principles. Such 'objects' cannot be experienced through the senses, they cannot be seen, touched or heard, but, for Plato, this did not imply that they were not real. We can see numerical symbols such as '2', '+' and '=', but we cannot actually see what these symbols mean: all we can do is to show that we know what the symbols mean by using them correctly. The crucial point for Plato is that words cannot be made to mean anything we want them to mean, *if* we want to make sense and to communicate. A language, according to Plato's theory, possesses a structure of rules and principles, the same structure as that of our system of ideas, but in the medium of signs that can be seen, heard and used. In the absence of this structure, real communication would be impossible: to repeat, 'any discourse we can have owes its existence to the weaving together of Forms' (*Sophist* 259e).

The fact that words and sentences can have objective meaning is important to us: it guarantees that words can have the same meaning for different people in different contexts of communication; it makes it possible for there to be a real difference between a true statement and one that is false, since a statement must first be meaningful if it is to be one or the other; and finally the fact that there can be such a thing as objective meaning makes it possible for us to resist the seductive words and images by which salesmen, advertisers, and, of course, ambitious politicians and their spin-doctors seek to manipulate our thoughts, tastes and behaviour.

The theory of ideas is important to Plato's view of knowledge. We will now leave the last word, perhaps a word of warning, to Plato.

Knowledge is what is of deep and permanent value for human beings, for understanding the world, for improving the moral quality of their individual lives, and for bringing about justice in society. How, then, would Plato have responded to the claim that we do in fact value knowledge very highly and base our plans and projects on what we know rather than what we happen to believe? This is an interesting question and concerns what Plato might have seen as an important difference between knowledge and information. From Plato's perspective knowledge has a value for human beings which mere information cannot have. Knowledge is necessarily of what is real and of serious and permanent value and the true statements that express this knowledge cannot be doubted or discarded. Information, on the other hand, even though we often have no choice but to rely on it, can be doubted and can, on occasion, turn out to be inaccurate or false and unimportant. We seek information for practical purposes and it derives its value from the importance we attach to those purposes. If we have been told to follow a strict programme of exercise for the sake of sporting success, for example, then we need information regarding that programme; if we are organizing a journey then we need to gather information regarding the departure and arrival of trains, the availability and price of accommodation, and so forth. Yet once the programme has served its purpose and the journey has been completed, the information, which may or may not have been reliable, is no longer of use and may be discarded. What Plato regarded as knowledge, in contrast to mere belief or practically useful data, cannot cease to be of value and cannot be discarded in the way that information often can.

Information can also be used to for the purpose of judging probabilities and making predictions. In order to make a wise rather than an arbitrary decision over which horse to bet on in a particular race I need information about the pedigree of the horse, its form, the condition of the ground, the ability of the trainer, and so forth. Alas, as so often with such probabilities and predictions, such decisions may turn out to be wrong. But knowledge, as Plato conceives it, cannot have this kind of predictive value. The rational character of practical decisions depends on the extent and reliability of the information at our disposal and in a culture dominated by quantitative ideas of value it is not at all surprising that information should be so highly valued in connection with consumer choices, financial affairs and strategic planning, both in personal life and in the formation of government policy. However, such information, which may in certain circumstances be complex and sophisticated, cannot deepen our understanding of reality, of moral value and of political justice, and, once achieved, cannot be ignored or discarded. It is true that in science observation and experiment provide the scientist with information, but this is valuable in the context of a theory that makes that information relevant and valuable. If the theory turns out to be false, the information ceases to be of value. Knowledge, for Plato, is knowledge of real ideas and what they mean and it is by understanding ideas that we come to understand what is important to us.

5

The soul: the search for mind and morality

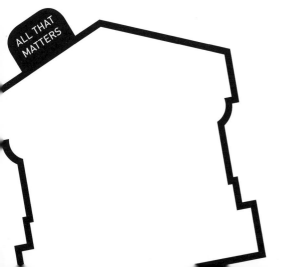

ALL THAT MATTERS

The Greek word *psyche* – always translated as 'soul' – figures so prominently in Plato's dialogues that it might well seem to be the idea that interested him most. Socrates had claimed that care of the soul should take priority over all other considerations in a person's life: Plato both accepted this principle and made the task of explaining the nature of the soul central to his inquiries. He came to see that understanding the soul had an unavoidable bearing on how we tackle all the major questions of philosophy – the real nature of the world, of knowledge, virtue and justice – and this led him to initiate what were to become two great traditions in the history of the discipline: first, an interest in human psychology which persists to the present day, and second, the theory of dualism according to which the minds and bodies of individual persons are essentially different in kind and, therefore, separate from each other, a theory which has interested modern philosophers as much as it did Plato. By uncovering what really matters in Plato's inquiries into the soul we will gain a greater understanding of his philosophy as a whole.

▶ The early theory

The *Phaedo*, a dialogue named after one of the characters who participates in the discussion, is one of the great works of the middle period of Plato's career. The setting of the dialogue is fascinating in that it imagines Socrates and a group of friends (although Plato himself is not one of them) in his cell awaiting execution by drinking hemlock. Perhaps unsurprisingly, the topic with which they begin is whether the soul survives death. Socrates begins by making the bold claim that he expects to be alive, as a soul, after he has died in a physical sense (*Phaedo* 63b–c). The discussion that follows gives a clear understanding of what Plato took the soul to be at this stage of his philosophical development. The idea that the soul survives the destruction of the body clearly implies that it is essentially different from the body; the fact that Socrates claims that the fate of those who have been morally good will be much better than the one suffered by those who have lived immoral lives indicates that, for Plato, the soul had a moral significance that the modern idea of the mind does not have. As we shall see, this is an immensely important idea in Plato's moral and political philosophy.

The first step Socrates takes in defending his claim is to define death. Instead of taking what was to become the modern way of treating death in physical and biological terms, Socrates describes it as the release of the soul from the body, a form of liberation to be welcomed rather than a cause of fear and regret. What then is the difference between the body and the soul to which, during the course of a person's life, it has been attached?

The body is a biological organism that, after conception, birth, growth and decline, finally ceases to function and dies; it is in contact with the physical world through sensory experiences; it is also what might be called the 'location' of desires, instincts and the feelings that we experience in various kinds of emotional reaction such as fear, anger, love and hate. Quite clearly the body, through desires, impulses and emotional reactions, inevitably influences the soul in ways that are, for Plato, almost always unfortunate and, if not resisted and checked, lead to wrongdoing and harm, both to other people and to the soul itself, to a person's failure to 'save' his or her life from moral harm and disaster (*Protagoras* 356d).

What, then, is the soul? It is not a physical entity (perhaps it should not be thought of as an entity at all), it is invisible, and cannot be destroyed in the ways that physical things can be destroyed, which implies, of course, that that it cannot die in the same way as a physical organism. In this dialogue the soul is understood in terms of its proper function, the capacity to reason and thus to achieve knowledge rather than mere belief, knowledge being the real source of wisdom, virtue and happiness in the lives of persons. The idea of the soul also includes our identities as persons (we retain the same identity after death as we had in life) as well as covering what we would now call a person's moral character, the kind of person someone is in a moral sense.

What follows from these differences? Quite simply the body, through desires, instincts and passions, can overwhelm the soul and thus cause forms of behaviour that, if unrestrained, inevitably harm the soul. The function of the soul, therefore, is to resist the influence of the body in order to maintain a person's moral well-being and happiness. Given that souls are immaterial and, therefore, cannot causally influence the body, how is this possible? On Plato's account it is by achieving knowledge that the soul can release itself from the destructive influence of desires and emotions: if a person is able to gain knowledge of what is authentically good, virtuous and valuable, rather than the counterfeit and illusory forms these may take, then that knowledge, by the authority of truth, will release the soul from the influence of the body. However, the body, through its experiences and desires, cannot itself be the source of that knowledge: whenever the soul 'attempts to investigate anything with the body, it is clearly deceived by it'; it is only 'in reasoning that any reality becomes clear to the soul' (*Phaedo* 65b–c), and reasoning is assumed to involve ideas or Forms, although at this stage Plato was not entirely clear about the nature of Forms or the way in which reasoning depends on them.

Plato's account of knowledge and virtue may be clarified with reference to the film *Double Indemnity*, a classic film noir directed by Billy Wilder and released in 1944. In brief, the story concerns a successful insurance salesman called Walter Kneff and what may be described in platonic terms as the destruction of his soul. He is easy-going in his outlook on life, not deeply reflective and thus vulnerable to the kind of temptation that leads to actions that, according to Plato in the *Phaedo*, inevitably damage a person's moral character. And so it proves. One day Walter, seeking the renewal of an insurance policy, goes to the house of a Mr and Mrs Dietrichson. Mrs Dietrichson answers the door and in a very short time Walter has become infatuated with her and has joined her in a plot to murder her husband so that they may collect and then enjoy the money for which he has been insured. Walter commits the murder but the plan goes badly wrong. He is betrayed by Mrs Dietrichson and both are fatally shot in their final confrontation. She dies instantly but Walter manages to drive back to his company office where he records his confession, which begins: 'I did it for the money and for a girl; I didn't get the money and I didn't get the girl.'

From the perspective of Plato's conception of the moral nature of the soul the point of the story is straightforward: by lacking the knowledge involved in virtue, Walter is unable to resist the allure of money and sexual attraction and is thus deluded into thinking that he can commit murder and fraud and still enjoy the happiness for which he committed them. When he does become aware of the damage his actions have inflicted on his soul it is too late: death releases the soul from the body but, in Walter's case, it is a morally damaged soul forever condemned to remain in that state. For Plato death is morally important because, when it comes, it fixes the moral state of the soul forevermore. It is only through depth of knowledge and understanding that individual persons can achieve moral harmony, and therefore genuine happiness, in their souls. This is portrayed in the *Phaedo* as a striving to free the soul as much as possible from the destructive influences of excessive desires, powerful emotions, and unrestrained impulses.

▶ The later theory

In his great and best-known work, the *Republic*, Plato takes the soul to be more complex, both in its internal structure and in its relationship to the social environment in which a person is situated, than the dualism of the

Phaedo. Plato remained convinced that the idea of the soul is essential to understanding the moral nature of persons and, indeed, that conflict is the key to explaining how the soul functions. But his attention now shifts from the conflict between body and soul to the conflicts that occur within the soul itself. In the *Republic* the soul of a human being is described as being made up of three parts, a change which brings with it a further difference that has an important bearing on a range of topics treated in the *Republic*: knowledge, moral virtue, political justice, citizenship, education and art.

In the *Republic*, Plato describes the soul as being composed of three parts or aspects. First, there is the 'appetite' that, as in the *Phaedo*, involves a person's desires and the actions that aim at their satisfaction. Then there is what Plato calls 'spirit', which is to be understood, not as spirituality, but as a person's natural tendency to defend himself, to 'stand up for himself', as well as his family, friends and community, in the face of physical threat, personal slander, humiliating treatment, and so forth. Finally, there is 'reason', the soul's capacity for logical thought, ultimately in pursuit of the knowledge and understanding necessary for maintaining order and harmony in the soul itself. As in his earlier account of the soul, desires and emotions are liable to run beyond a person's control and disrupt the soul's inner harmony. Yet how reason is to curb excessive desires and the aggressive and violent impulses of the spirited part is not made entirely clear. What is now clear is that Plato sees the soul as being permanently placed in a social environment and that it is a person's interactions with that environment that are ultimately the source of the inner conflicts that damage and destroy a person's moral character. In this sense, the relationship between body and soul that was central to the *Phaedo* is now replaced by the relationship between the soul and the society to which a person belongs. The soul is particularly vulnerable to such conflicts in unjust societies, in tyrannies, military dictatorships, oligarchies and the kind of democracy by which Athens was ruled during Plato's lifetime. The moral culture characteristic of an unjust society will pull individual persons away from the forms of knowledge and virtue that promote and sustain justice. Justice exists in a person's soul when reason is in control: by exercising its authority and influence reason is able to ensure that each part of the soul, including itself, functions in accordance with its own characteristic virtue rather than being undermined by the vice to which it is vulnerable: moderation (rather than excess) in the case of desire; courage (rather than uncontrolled aggression and recklessness) in the case of spirit; knowledge, intelligence and wisdom (rather than ignorance and folly) in the case of reason itself. By maintaining the presence and co-operation of these three great qualities in the soul, reason ensures that it is in a state of harmony and happiness.

However, the soul does not exist in isolation. Human beings interact with each other in many ways and in many settings and are so deeply embedded in a society and its culture that there is, Plato believed, an inevitable and close relationship between the moral condition of individual souls and the moral, cultural and political ethos of the society in which they live. Individual happiness, for Plato, is entirely dependent on whether individuals live in a just society, one that is appropriately ordered and wisely governed.

To summarize, Plato continued to believe throughout his career that the soul, and thus the psychology of persons, possessed an essentially moral nature (the most popular view now is that human psychology is computational and mechanical in character) and that the true function of reason, as the soul's principal capacity, was to secure and maintain its virtuous and just character and its expression in a person's actions. However, during the course of his long working life Plato's views on the nature of the soul changed and so did his understanding of how a person's moral character can be developed and sustained. In the *Phaedo* he had assumed that Socrates had been right to insist that by achieving knowledge of the virtues and their importance the soul would free itself from the power of desire. In the *Republic*, however, soul and human psychology in general are seen to be more complex. Although a person's virtue and happiness remain of the highest importance, Plato no longer viewed these in terms of a single kind of conflict between the soul and the causal influence of the body. In the *Republic* the need to resolve the conflicts that destroy the inner harmony of the soul are to be understood in relation to the ways in which the lives of individuals, and more precisely their moral understanding and sensibility, are shaped by the society and culture in which those lives are pursued. It is in connection with this more complex view of the soul that Plato inquires into the relationship between the possibility of human goodness and happiness and the nature of political justice.

6

Philosophy and justice: the search for happiness

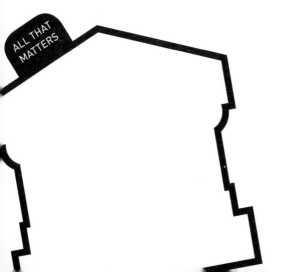
ALL THAT MATTERS

Plato's *Republic* is one of the great books of human history. As in the great majority of Plato's dialogues Socrates is the leading character in the discussion and, although a wide range of topics are considered, all of them are connected with the aim of developing a full and convincing account of justice. It all begins with an interesting question: can justice be recommended for its own sake as well as for the practical and material benefits it brings to human beings? For Socrates, if there is such a thing as real justice then it should be possible to justify it in its own right, in accordance with its own internal principles, and to communicate its meaning and authority. As I have suggested, much of Plato's work is, at least implicitly, concerned with authority and the *Republic* may be read as a search for the meaning and authority of justice. The challenge Socrates is to meet is set out very clearly by Thrasymachus, a participant in the early part of the dialogue. In a statement that dramatically anticipates a view that was to become common in modern times, Thrasymachus declares that the very idea of real justice is meaningless; justice is relative, it has no fixed form and meaning; it varies from one society to another but in all its forms it is always determined by the interests of the stronger party in that society, the party with power to maintain its own advantage. For Socrates, however, this can only mean that there is no such thing as justice at all and he sets about meeting Thrasymachus' challenge by constructing an elaborate account of what, in practice, a just society would involve.

▲ An Athenian-style democratic assembly

▶ The central argument

At the heart of Plato's inquiry is the relationship between a person's soul and the society to which that person belongs. It is not surprising, of course, that Plato should have been aware of this: there clearly is a relationship between what human beings are like, what they value, what they believe, what they aspire to, and so forth, and the kind of society and culture to which they belong. However, the principle by which he explains this relationship is striking: the structure of society is exactly the same as the structure of the individual soul (*Republic* 441c–e). A society, like an individual person, has material needs that must be met: the need for food, clothing and shelter and the tools with which to work. Again, like the individual, a community is vulnerable to external attack and, therefore, in need of adequate protection. And finally, just as an individual needs proper self-government to bring about harmony and well-being, so wise government is required to maintain justice, and thus to promote happiness, for the community as a whole.

Although the theory is not without difficulty, its main point is of great interest. There is a close and inevitable relationship between the condition of a person's soul – whether that person is virtuous and happy – and the character of the cultural ethos (what individuals are encouraged to believe, to value and devote their energy) by which that person is influenced.

How does Plato explain this? As we have already mentioned, the relationship between body and soul as it was understood in the *Phaedo* is replaced in the *Republic* by the relationship between individual people and the kind of society into which they are born, grow to maturity and pursue their lives. In short, the conflicts that cause disharmony within the soul are the result of injustice in society, itself a matter of conflict and disharmony caused by flawed institutions, inappropriate laws, and unjust and bad government.

The key to the parallel between the parts of the soul and the parts of society are the ideas of virtue and justice. Each part of the soul, as we have seen, is understood by reference to a specific human need and a distinction between the virtue and the vice connected with that need and its satisfaction. A person is virtuous and happy when, through the controlling authority of reason, the appropriate virtues – wisdom, courage and moderation – are dominant in each part of the soul. The same consideration holds for society: a society is harmonious in the way that justice demands when intelligent and wise government ensures that society as a whole is moderate rather than excessive in material and commercial life and courageous and competent in matters of security and defence. If these virtues can be established in society as a whole then the aim of justice, that of ensuring happiness, which is *not* 'the disproportional happiness of any one class in society but the greatest happiness of the whole' (Republic 420b), will have been achieved. It is a commendable aim: who could deny that working towards the most equal distribution of happiness in society is a good thing? But can it be achieved?

Plato's positive answer, although we might find it initially surprising, can seem rather attractive. A just society will be one in which exactly the right kind of relationship holds between the order and harmony within individual souls and the order and harmony of society. In both spheres of life, order is maintained by the control exercised by reason, intelligence and wisdom over desire and spirit. And the consequences of justice will be considerable: if a society is organized in the way justice demands, and also ruled by people of the highest intelligence and integrity, then the maximum number of citizens will be free from the obstacles that stand in the way of personal virtue, the temptations and distractions that create merely the illusion rather than the reality of happiness, a condition of soul that can only be achieved through the discipline of reason and knowledge.

How then should a just society be organized? The answer Plato offers turns on the fundamental principle of justice: in a just society it will be essential that each individual citizen, both male and female (for, contrary to the actual laws of the Athenian constitution, women will be full citizens in Plato's just society) 'dedicate himself to the single task for which he is naturally suited.' As we now know, Plato regarded unity and order (understood in terms of moral values and virtues) as the hallmarks of justice and the 'principle of specialization', as we may call it, was to ensure both that each individual person would be a unity rather than a plurality of conflicting parts and that the community they belonged to would be a stable, harmonious and unified. The structure of a just society can only be sustained if individual citizens confine themselves to the kind of work for which they are naturally suited, to the responsibilities that go with that role, and, more broadly, to the way of life they will enjoy within a particular social group. But they will have been placed in that group, not by virtue of birth or wealth and property, but through the education and training by which their natural aptitudes and abilities have been identified and developed. Most important of all, Plato argues, this principle of specialization leads to the conclusion that the distinctive

▲ Plato's allegory of The Cave

unity and order of a just society can only be achieved and sustained by specialists in the art of government, qualified for this responsibility by intellect, moral character and temperament and the appropriate kind of education. Only by their dedication to this task, rather than furthering the advantages of any one section of society, can the happiness of the maximum number of individuals be achieved. We will develop this further in the next chapter.

▶ Inside the Cave

We will now return to Plato's interest in the connections between society, media and politics. Plato exploits a number of powerful images in defending his conception of justice. The most striking, and famous, of these is the image of the Cave, an uncanny anticipation of the manner in which the public culture of modern society has come to be increasingly dominated by the screen and the forms of media placed on it: the cinema, the television, the computer and the tablet. The purpose of Plato's image is to represent the condition of human life in the unjust societies that Plato condemned for their damaging effects on the thought, sensibility and behaviour of individual citizens: tyranny, oligarchy, military rule, and, of course, Athenian democracy. This is the image:

'Here is a situation you can use as an analogy for the human condition – for our education or lack of it. Imagine people living in a cavernous cell down under the ground; at the far end of the cave, a long way off, there's an entrance open to the outside world. They've been there since childhood, with their necks and legs tied up in a way which keeps them in one place and allows them to look only straight ahead and not to turn their heads. There's firelight burning a long way

further up the cave behind them, and up the slope between the fire and the prisoners there's a road, beside which you should imagine a low wall has been built – like the partition which conjurors place between themselves and their audience and above which they show their tricks. Imagine also that there are people on the other side of this wall who are carrying all sorts of artefacts. These artefacts, human statuettes, and animal models carved in stone and wood and all kinds of materials stick out over the wall; and as you expect, some of the people talk as they carry these objects along, while others are silent.'

(Republic 514a–15a)

Such people are no different to the people of Athens, Socrates explains; they do not see anything of themselves and each other but are forced to spend their lives watching the shadows cast on the wall of the cave.

Plato created this image to support an important claim concerning the political aspect of media. It is not that human beings in their daily lives are forever seeing images on a screen, although in contemporary society many individuals do spend much of their time in front of screens of one kind or another, both in their work and in the entertainment that takes up a large part of their leisure time. Plato's point is that in unjust societies the perceptions, beliefs, values, purposes, interests and tastes of individual citizens are overwhelmingly conditioned by the images, whether in language or in other forms of media, that dominate their culture. For Plato this is a form of imprisonment that, through the manipulation of belief, desire and behaviour, deprives human beings of the freedom that can only be achieved through knowledge of what is real and genuinely valuable. The fact that the audience Plato imagines are prisoners chained in front of the screen, and thus forced to look at moving images intentionally projected on to the screen, suggests an important feature of the injustice Plato's image is meant to explain: like the verbal skills taught by the Sophists, the array of images placed on the wall of the cave is intended to persuade people to accept the beliefs, values and purposes that those in power, and those who control the media, want them to. Totalitarian regimes invariably seek to influence belief and behaviour by manipulating all forms of media, by controlling information, and by perverting artistic and educational practices for the purpose of indoctrination. Those who have been ready to accuse Plato of defending a form of totalitarianism have ignored the fact that the image of the Cave may be interpreted as a powerful condemnation of totalitarian regimes and the political practices and techniques by which the people in those regimes are deprived of knowledge and freedom.

But are we forever condemned to this kind of bondage? No, the great majority of citizens may, at least partially, be released from the illusions of the screen even though it is unlikely that many of them will be able to face and comprehend reality in the fullest sense, the world illuminated by the dazzling sunlight outside the cave. Plato concludes his narrative by imagining a small number of individuals who have been able to face and come to understand the real nature of the world and thus gain the kind of knowledge required for just government, returning to the Cave to take care of the souls of those who remain vulnerable to the manipulation and exploitation that inevitably go on in unjust societies. These will, of course, be the Guardians, the philosophically and morally educated individuals who have been able to comprehend the Forms and thus the real nature of the world and that of a just society. The Guardians will be appropriately educated for their role and will be, in moral character and personal temperament, very different from corrupt tyrants, oligarchs and the democratic leaders who manipulate the Assembly by the techniques of oratory. It is crucially important that they should not be motivated by individual advantage, that their policies and decisions should not further the interests of a particular section of society, and that they should be entirely free from personal corruption.

The virtue and dedication of these leaders will have two sources: an education which leads to knowledge and wisdom in the highest degree, and the way of life prescribed for them, one that from the perspective of contemporary politics may seem most unattractive. Although those who are naturally marked out for guardianship will be the best minds of the community and fully qualified to transform the society of the Cave into one of justice and harmony, Plato believed that, because of the rewarding nature of philosophical thought and the sense of responsibility it fostered, they would be happy to accept this. And yet it seems that he was not entirely convinced of this and, for that reason, set out a number of conditions that would form a more practical obstacle to compromise and corruption. The Guardians will not be paid for their work, they will not own property (apart from bare essentials), they will not marry and enjoy family life, and they will live in a community of their own resembling both an academic college and a military barracks: the temptations that lead to political compromise and corruption are very great – wealth, family ambitions and class interests – and, Plato insists (with considerable irony and humour), that every possible measure must be taken to ensure that these temptations shall not arise.

But what about the other sections of society? The way of life that both the auxiliaries and the working craftsmen and producers will enjoy would seem to be far more normal and attractive than that of the Guardians and there is no reason to suppose that their lives would inevitably be dull, tedious and frustrating. If the social and economic order described in the *Republic* functions as it ought to, the individuals who live and work within these groups should be able to enjoy the satisfactions of their own abilities and skills, of contributing to the overall good of their community, and to enjoy the forms of entertainment and pleasure available to them. But what will these be? As we shall see in connection with Plato's discussion of education and art, the activities and forms of entertainment that individuals will pursue during their leisure time will be carefully selected and supervised by the Guardians; there will be no return to the shallow and mindless culture of the Cave. Furthermore, in spite of the fact that the society fashioned in the *Republic* is structured into three sectors, it will not be a society divided into three classes in the modern sense, which means, of course, that there will be no social mobility in the modern sense either, the kind of social movement that many individuals pursue by achieving professional status, by means of wealth, and by adopting the attitudes, tastes and aspirations of the class they seek to join. The social scheme articulated in the *Republic* is to be determined entirely by natural capacities and aptitudes, not by birth or wealth. It will be a society of equal citizenship (and thus of equal status), not one of class superiority. The scheme also articulates a radical conception of justice by identifying equality of opportunity as a crucial principle according to which individual persons, including women, may be prepared for life and work in any one of the three sectors of society; surely the very idea that women are, apart from physical strength, equal to men and may, if suitably qualified and educated, become Guardians, must have seemed a startling proposal at a time when traditional social roles were still deeply entrenched in Athenian culture.

Could such a society ever be established? And if it could be established, would it retain the form described in the *Republic*? Socrates concedes in the course of the dialogue that the likelihood of a truly just society being brought into existence is remote. It is rare for a society to present a blank slate for its rulers and transforming a society from a state of injustice into the kind of structure described in the *Republic* is impossible without causing immense disruption and harm. As it is, Plato is presenting us with a 'model', the form and details of which challenge us to subject the institutions, laws, practices and values of our own society to serious critical scrutiny. But the most interesting question is the second. Plato seems to have assumed that should such a state ever come about it would, nevertheless, be immensely difficult to prevent it from collapsing into the forms of injustice it was designed to overcome. For this reason Plato insisted that all necessary measures should be taken to prevent this from happening, including the use of myths, particularly that of 'the noble lie', to persuade citizens to accept the social order by which justice is to be maintained. According to this myth, all individual persons are born with a higher quantity of a particular metal in their souls than of the other metals. Some are born with more gold in their souls (potential Guardians), others with more silver (potential auxiliaries), and others with more bronze (potential craftsmen, workers and businessmen). The function of this 'story' is to persuade citizens to accept without question what we would now call the 'genetic' foundation for the social and political structure described in the *Republic*. It is a puzzling feature of Plato's inquiry that seems to imply that Plato was, after all his criticisms of rhetoric and oratory, prepared to accept that those very practices could, even though intellectually and morally flawed, serve the purpose of maintaining a just society.

7

Education and justice: the search for citizenship

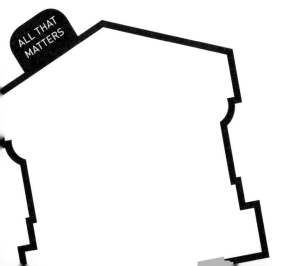
ALL THAT MATTERS

Plato introduced so many ideas, arguments and topics into philosophy for the first time that it should not surprise us that he was the first philosopher to think seriously about education and its connections with personal virtue, social justice, and the nature of citizenship. We should not be surprised either that his enquiries into education were exceptionally original and radical in the context of Athenian society and the wider world of Greek civilization. What passed for education at the time was rather haphazard and inadequate and wholly private, often conducted by slaves belonging to particular households. But increased commercial activity, growing prosperity and, by Greek standards, a large empire, brought new needs and the Sophists offered something of value to rather older citizens, a curriculum centred on the skills of what we have called 'life management' which included the techniques of oratory that would be of advantage to the pursuit of individual success and prosperity. Because Plato saw what he called the 'image-making' of the Sophists as furthering injustice rather than contributing to its eradication, he set himself the task of showing what the nature and aims of education ought to be in a just society. Because the Sophists were only concerned with persuasion, with bringing about conviction rather than knowledge, they should not be regarded as teachers and educators at all. For Plato, the ultimate aim of education is to sustain a just society and, for that reason, he argued, education, properly understood, is only possible in a just society.

The importance Plato attached to education cannot be overestimated. Given that a just society is ordered for the purpose of promoting virtue and happiness in

▲ Illustrated vase showing Student at a Greek stone tablet

the lives of citizens, then, Plato argued, education will be the means by which that order is established and maintained. But the nature of the education designed to achieve that purpose will differ radically from the private, fragmented and inadequate forms of education that prevailed in Plato's Athens. It will be compulsory, its curriculum will be carefully selected and arranged, and the whole system will be rigorously supervised by those in political authority. We have only to remind ourselves that primary education was not made compulsory in Britain until 1870 and secondary was not available to all children until 1944 to realize just how radical Plato's proposals actually were.

Education, as we noted in the last chapter, is to play a vital role in maintaining the social structure required by justice; it will be the principal means by which individuals will be selected and prepared for the work they will carry out in particular sections of society. These will not be classes in the modern sense and individuals will not be placed in them by virtue of birth, wealth or power but rather by education: it is only education that can ensure that 'every person is not a plurality but a unity' and that 'the community as a whole will be a unity' (Republic 423c–d). As we noted in the last chapter the idea of specialized capacities and aptitudes is so important to Plato that he regarded it as nothing less than the foundation of a just society:

'Then this is what justice is. Here is an alternative way of putting it. Isn't it the case that when each of the three classes – the one that works for a living, the auxiliaries, and the Guardians – performs its proper function and does its own job in the community, then this is justice and makes the community a just one.'

(Republic 434c)

This is the principle that underlies Plato's boldest claim in the *Republic*, that the unity and order of a just society can only be maintained if it is ruled by a group of individuals – the Guardians of the community – who have been specially educated to perform this role by virtue of intellect, moral character and temperament. However, although the highest level of education will be directed to the selection and preparation of potential Guardians, the system of education will not serve them alone: there will be no individual in the community who will be deprived of an appropriate form of education (Republic 424a–c). The general aim of education in a just society is the moral development of all individual citizens.

Given that 'the same principles which exist in the state also exist in the individual soul' (*Republic* 441c), and that in both cases justice is a matter of unity and harmony maintained by the rule of reason over desire and spirit, how did Plato understand the education required to produce just citizens for a just society? His enquiry turns on the assumption that that not all individuals are born with the same aptitudes and propensities, certainly not to the same degree. Quite simply, some children are born with a greater capacity for rational thought or intelligence than other individuals who may have inherited either the personal qualities associated with spirit or the practical aptitudes that suit a person for skilled and productive work. It is these differences that are the likely source of conflict and injustice and, for Plato it will be the task of education to balance and harmonize them, both in the individual and the community.

Plato's arguments in defence of his theory are complex and not entirely sound: it is simply not the case, for example, that a person born with strong desires will also have a propensity for the skills of craftsmanship, productive work and ability in commercial affairs. But the essence of Plato's theory is this: education can only succeed in fostering good citizenship, and thus promote a just society, by bringing about moral unity and order in individual souls, and it can only do this by ensuring that the virtues of moderation, courage and wisdom, in both the soul and the state, prevail over the vices of excess, cowardice and folly. And, as we already know, those virtues will depend on reason, with its own virtue of wisdom, being in control. It is at this point that the relationship between the individual soul and the authority of government fits into place in practical terms. Plato made the crucial observation that there are some individuals, perhaps a majority, who will not be able to achieve self-restraint, whether in terms of desire or the tendencies of aggression and violence, by themselves. And he concludes, therefore, that it will be one of the principal tasks of just government to ensure that this restraint prevails not only through wise guardianship and legislation but ultimately through a properly organized system of education. In brief, skilled and productive workers will live temperate lives devoted to the tasks and practices to which they are naturally suited and which have been developed by their education and training; the members of the group of auxiliaries who represent the spirited aspect of the community, will possess the virtues of bravery and honour appropriate to their role; and the Guardians, by virtue of their capacity for rational thought and their prolonged and rigorous education, will take responsibility for ruling with wisdom and authority.

Before we look at the kind of education Plato recommended, both the specialized and advanced education of the Guardians and the general curriculum for the community as a whole, we must note that Plato's vision of the role education is to play in a just society contains a number of radical features. The first, as we have already mentioned, is that the Guardians, quite unlike contemporary politicians, will not own property or be allowed to accumulate wealth: guardianship, as Plato conceived it, must be free from all temptation to corruption. For that reason Plato also denied them the right to marry and have families: families, then as now, particularly wealthy and aristocratic families, can be powerful centres of interest that can contribute decisively to social division, disunity and injustice. But it is the third feature that is the most surprising. One of the principal elements in Plato's conception of justice is what we now call equality of opportunity, something to which education is vitally important. If the children of craftsmen, workers, soldiers and administrators have the appropriate qualities for guardianship then they will be given the education that will equip them for that role. And it follows, of course, that if children produced by the Guardians (who will enjoy sexual relations, although not in the context of a family) do not have the appropriate qualities for government they will take their place in either the productive sector or in the ranks of the auxiliaries. And Plato goes against the grain of traditional Athenian custom in granting the opportunity to guardianship, and thus to the appropriate education, to women as well as men: with the exception of minor differences such as physical strength, Plato defended the equality of men and women as citizens who make an active and positive contribution to a just community. We may appreciate the radical nature of this proposal by reminding ourselves that in Athenian society women, in company with slaves and resident foreign workers, did not enjoy citizenship and, outside the rearing of young children and the management of households, played little role in the life of the community. Given that in our own society the right to vote was not granted to all women above the age of 21 until 1928 and that Britain did not have a female Prime Minister until 1979, Plato was far ahead of his time.

Finally, what kind of education does Plato recommend for his just society? The ultimate aim of government in Plato's just society is freedom from the illusions of the Cave. To be able to work towards that end the Guardians themselves must be free from the illusions and the shallow and superfluous desires that are forced upon individual mentality by the culture of an unjust society. It is by means of another important image, that of the Divided Line, that Plato clarifies how this freedom can be achieved. As shown below we are to imagine a vertical line representing a division between two realms.

The purpose of the line is to represent four stages of intellectual and moral growth. Although it might seem paradoxical, the 'higher' a person is able to ascend the line the deeper that person's knowledge and understanding becomes. Each side begins at the lowest level and ends at the highest. On one side of the line are placed the 'objects' that human beings experience and know with varying degrees of clarity and certainty, e.g. images and shadows such as the silhouettes on the wall of the Cave on the lowest level and the Forms that are the 'objects' of real knowledge and understanding on the highest level. On the other side of the line are placed the capacities by which the soul is in contact with those 'objects', sense experience in the case of physical objects, visible images and shadows at the lowest level and the rational thought by which the Forms are known and understood at the highest. It is, of course, the Forms that are most important for the education of the Guardians, the real and objective ideas that are

Experience and cognition	Degrees of clarity and certainty
A. Knowledge	Forms
B. Thought and reasoning	Symbols and signs, e.g. the symbols of mathematics and logic
C. Belief and guesswork	Physical objects, qualities, events and processes
D. Sense, perception and imagination	Images, shadows, reflections
A – B: The realm of truth and knowledge	
C – D: The realm of visual appearances	

discovered rather than created by human beings: quite unlike the particular things in the world that resemble them, the Forms themselves are not subject to change and modification; and, in contrast to the objects we experience, Forms are absolutely clear and can be fully understood, both in themselves and in relation to other Forms, 'by the eye of the soul' (Republic 510e). Developing the ability to understand the meanings contained in Forms is the final and absolutely necessary stage in the Guardians' education: it is only from this perspective that they will be able to understand the ideas of goodness and justice that are to guide them in the tasks of legislating and educating for a just society.

The images of the Cave and the Line are immensely important to how Plato understands the relationships that ought to hold between education, citizenship and justice. Whereas the image of the Cave conveys our condition prior to liberation from illusions, fantasies and shallow desires, the image of the Line expresses the structure and content of the education ultimately necessary for good government. However, it is also important to see that these images are not exclusively concerned with the most advanced stages of education. A society can only be just if education influences the souls of all its citizens and the crucial point of the image of the Cave is that in a just society no one needs to be chained before the screen for their entire lives. Because not everyone inherits the same characteristics, and because different abilities and skills are required for different roles, not everyone in the new community will receive the same kind of education. Nevertheless, everyone will receive an education, in such fields as the crafts, gymnastics and music, which is designed to free them from the illusions, desires and habits that stand in the way of the virtue and happiness at which education should be directed. (Plato introduces the grim thought – seriously? – that anyone who fails to respond to their education will be put to death (Republic 409e–10a). The education of the Guardians takes longer than that of the auxiliaries and the craftsmen and producers, but they too will live good and valuable lives by virtue of being educated in a society to which they will dedicate their lives.

Plato's picture of education and justice in the *Republic* is provocative and challenging. It is impossible to deny that education should serve the best interests of individuals and play a major role in sustaining a just society; neither can it be denied that the primary aim of what goes on in educational settings is to liberate individuals from what would harm them intellectually and morally. And yet there now seems to be great uncertainty over what the real aims of education actually are. This, for Plato, would be a matter for concern and should be given serious thought. Furthermore, he would also encourage educationalists to think carefully about the importance he attached to moral education and the kind of preparation required for citizenship in a just society: justice and citizenship are so closely related that real citizenship, which depends crucially on the appropriate education, is itself only possible in a justly ordered and well-governed society. At a time in which our public and political culture is dominated by monetary and market values, education has come to be seen as a process of acquiring skills and qualifications and higher education as a commercial investment on the part of students who hope to achieve the kind of success in life that make their investment worthwhile. Although Plato certainly did not exclude practical abilities and skills from the education he outlines in the *Republic*, he might well have regarded the current state of British education, with its limited concern for moral and cultural development and the requirements of citizenship in our liberal democracy, as misdirected and impoverished. We will allow Plato himself to make further comments on this in the next chapter.

8

Art and society:
the search for truth

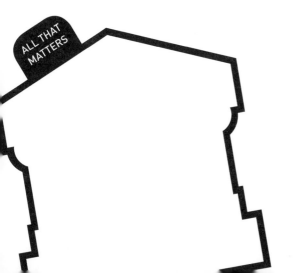

ALL THAT
MATTERS

Understanding the world through art is impossible: forms of art, according to Plato, are essentially instances of image-making and thus comparable to the practice of oratory. Oratory is always dangerous but art, whether in the form of poetry, drama, painting, sculpture or music, is image-making that can be useful as well as dangerous. Why?

Art is ubiquitous. Beginning in prehistoric times, the creation, display and performance of works of art is a striking feature of very many societies and cultures, serving important functions within particular forms of life. And, as Plato was very aware, forms of art such as imaginative writing, painting, modelling, dramatic enactment and music-making can feature prominently in a person's education, particularly in its early stages. We have been aware throughout our discussion that Plato attached the greatest importance to reality rather than appearance, to the real nature of physical things, communication, virtue, justice, education and citizenship. We have also seen that his ultimate concern was the moral condition of the human soul and the real happiness that is available to human beings as citizens of a just society. We might have assumed, therefore, that art, which in all its forms involves appearances, whether in language, visual images or sound, would have been peripheral to his philosophical concerns. This was certainly not the case: throughout his career Plato was intensely interested in – even obsessed by – the nature of art and the powerful influence works of art could have on individual mentality and public culture. The fact that works of art are created in particular kinds of media implies that artistic media are also open to the abuses that can be made of any kind of medium, to deceive, manipulate and persuade rather than enlighten through the communication of truth. Quite clearly the creation of art and its function in society had, for Plato, a close affinity with the ideas and practices of the Sophists. It is against this background that we must look at Plato's interest in art.

Art can be a serious threat to justice and human well-being as well as valuable to the education of young people. But even in the context of education the use of art must be handled with great care. Young people are impressionable and they are susceptible to undesirable influences from an early age, influences that, as Plato realized, could distort their moral development and mar their adult lives. Therefore, artistic creation, just like a society's economic affairs, must be 'regulated' by those in authority; the character of acceptable forms of poetry, drama, visual art and music must be carefully set out and supervised according to appropriate aims and standards.

At first, Plato seems to value art very highly. It must, of course, be the right kind of art and it must be rigorously supervised: just as those who work in the field of commerce and finance will always be tempted to make easy money by ignoring rules and laws, so artists, it seems, will also be perennially tempted to create works of art that are not conducive to personal well-being and social harmony. Young people in the community should be encouraged to cultivate such qualities as the good use of language, grace, elegance, harmony and rhythm because these can be allied with moral goodness and excellence (*Republic* 400d–e). Painting,

▲ Greek vase

sculpture, weaving, embroidery and manufactured objects, as well as natural structures, animals and plants, may all display grace and elegance and may be rightly appreciated and valued. But, as Plato so often pointed out, the opposite qualities are also possible: 'inelegance, lack of rhythm, and disharmony are allied to abuse of language and corrupt character, whereas their opposites are allied to and reflect a disciplined and good character' (*Republic* 401a). Art is morally significant, it can work for what is bad as well as what is good, and its dangers are too great for artistic creation and its impact upon individuals and public culture to be left to the artists themselves and those who commission and exploit their work. In Plato's just society poets will be made to choose either to represent goodness rather than meanness of spirit and inelegance in their creations or to refrain completely from practising their art. The work of artists and artisans in general must, then, be carefully supervised to make sure that young people must not be surrounded by 'images of badness' that they are likely to absorb into their souls: just as art is imitative so art itself can be imitated, for the bad as well as the good. Plato is eloquent on this:

'We must look for craftsmen who have the innate gift for tracking down goodness and grace, so that the young people of our community can live in a salubrious region *where everything is beneficial and where their eyes and ears meet no influence except those of fine works of art, whose effect is like a breeze which brings health from favourable regions, and which imperceptibly guides them, from childhood onwards, until they are assimilated to, familiar with, and in harmony with the beauty of reason.'*

(Republic 401c–d)

The claim Plato is making here is that works of art, by being in harmony with reason, are also in conformity with reality, even though, because they are composed of images, those artistic forms can never actually represent and comprehend reality in the way that only the correct application of ideas through language can.

Art, then, can be immensely beneficial in a person's moral and cultural education, in the development of good taste and in fostering appreciation of real value: good art nourishes the moral growth and health of the soul; bad art does the exact opposite, stunting moral growth and warping our capacity to appreciate what is fine and beautiful, what a modern philosopher would call our aesthetic sensibility. The function of good art, the art that is of value in a just society, is to 'humanize', to cultivate virtuous character and moral sensitivity as well as good taste in poetry, visual art and music. It is clear, however, that such art will only be possible if artists are able to make their creations and compositions conform to the virtues of self-restraint, courage, integrity, generosity, and so forth. Art, like a good teacher, must set a good example and not pander to morally deplorable traits of character and behaviour. This means, of course, that the works of art that will gain approval in a just society are not to be judged in terms of their own purely artistic features: Plato might well have agreed with Oscar Wilde's statement (in *The Picture of Dorian Gray*) that 'All art is at once surface and symbol' but not with Wilde's further statement that 'All art is quite useless'. The forms of art that will be judged acceptable, both in educational practice and in the wider culture of society, should represent things realistically and positively; they should represent virtuous character and conduct as attractive so that they may be imitated by individuals for the good of their souls. In short, for Plato art is to serve the same purpose as education in general, which is the moral growth of personal character.

What Plato was advocating is not, of course, very different from a principle followed in all systems of education, that the content of a curriculum must be carefully selected and arranged so that educational aims may be achieved to the greatest possible extent. And although the content and methods of education may serve a number of different aims, for Plato their primary aim was the moral and personal maturity of citizens in a just society: in unjust societies – Germany under Hitler and the Nazi Party and the Soviet Union under Stalin's tyranny come to mind – education simply cannot serve that purpose. Our ideas concerning education and the social function of art may differ from Plato's, but the relationships he forged between art, education and citizenship (*good* citizenship in a completely just society rather than the compromised status of individuals in tyrannies, oligarchies and military dictatorships) are surely commendable: it is only in a just society that the lives of individual citizens can be given substantial meaning and the right kind of moral and cultural direction.

However, it must also be said that Plato's views on art are limited and puzzling. Most parents in contemporary societies are careful about the kinds of art and media with which their children have contact, which shows that, like Plato, many people believe that some forms of art can be harmful while others are of positive value. When art glamorizes violence, crime, sexual promiscuity, drug abuse, and so forth, both parents and politicians are concerned because glamour can render certain kinds of attitude and behaviour attractive and influential. Art can be created to pander to unpleasant and dangerous features of human character and action: egoism, selfishness, vanity, ruthlessness, aggression, violence, and so forth, the tendencies and impulses that good education should, according to Plato, work against. And yet, in spite of these 'Platonic' anxieties and recommendations regarding the misuse of artistic and other media, it is clear that Plato's views on art are in some respects flawed. He is unable to see how works of art of the highest quality, such as epic poetry, tragic drama, the visual arts, and even music, all of which he was familiar with, may deepen our understanding of human life by conveying insights into personal psychology, the nature of human relationships and the complexity of moral and emotional life, not by avoiding the representation of immorality and corruption but by representing them in the kind of depth that is one of the defining features of good and great art. It is this blind spot that limits Plato's understanding of art, which in turn limits the kind of art to which he could give his approval.

Plato returns to the topic of art in the final book of the *Republic*, but now his attitude towards art seems to have hardened. Although some socially useful forms of art may be retained because they reinforce morally desirable qualities of character and encourage virtuous conduct – 'hymns to the gods' and 'eulogies to the people' are the examples mentioned – the danger of 'falling under the spell of poetry' is so great that the wisest policy would be to banish poets from the community altogether: censorship with a vengeance. Poetry, like all art, is concerned with appearances and appearances are intrinsically deceptive and manipulative. Only art that represents the virtues as attractive and admirable, and thus encourages individuals to shape their lives by the virtues, is to be tolerated and even that must be diligently supervised. This is not, for Plato, a trivial matter:

'What's in the balance is absolutely crucial, far more than people think. Its whether one becomes a good person or a bad person, and consequently has the calibre not to be distracted by prestige, wealth, political power, or even poetry from applying one self to morality and whatever else goodness involves.'

(Republic 608b)

What, then, is Plato's major challenge concerning art and its relation to society? Even though in the *Laws*, a late work concerned more with practical political policy than with the ideal of justice, Plato finds a place for works of art that give 'innocent pleasure' (*Laws* 670d), he retains the view that the art that is of value must be morally educative and, as such, must conform to truth rather than pretend to discover and express it. Plato's challenge is that we should look carefully and critically at the art that figures prominently in our society, the art that is popular as well as the art that is judged to be complex, sophisticated and serious. What does this art tell us about the character of our public culture and about our interests and tastes as individuals? We should also consider what these forms of art tell us about the motives and values of those who create, sponsor and present forms of art in our society. Is there, as Plato thought, a relationship between the forms of art to which individuals are attracted and their effect on their moral character and their attitudes and behaviour towards others? Finally, we should consider carefully the political aspect of artistic media with a view to identifying the political exploitation of art that may be damaging to the structure and the moral and cultural ethos of the kind of liberal democracy that, after serious reflection on the alternatives, we may wish to retain and restore to its real nature.

9

Epilogue:
Plato now

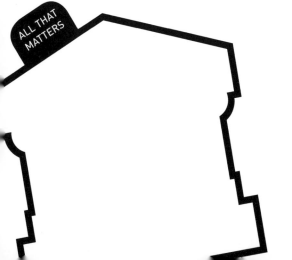

We have argued throughout this book that Plato's philosophy matters, not just because it shapes the whole history of the subject, but also because of its value for understanding the problems we face in our own society at the present time. We are not required to accept his views as right but they do challenge us to consider very seriously the values we uncritically live by and the purposes we pursue with little concern for their real worth. We now have a good understanding of Plato's most fundamental ideas and concerns: it is against that background that we will conclude our study by imagining how Plato might have responded to some of the most prominent features of our social and political culture into which our lives are woven.

▶ Self-understanding and moral value

Understanding our nature as souls or persons was, for Plato, a matter of great importance and one of the central tasks of philosophy. Plato might well have asked of us: just what do we take ourselves to be as persons? His answer is unlikely to have been flattering. The way in which many people understand themselves in contemporary society, even though their beliefs may not be clearly articulated, reflects the fact that their values, purposes and tasks are shaped in accordance with the assumptions that underlie free-market capitalism and the cultural and political ethos it inevitably generates. The great influence of the ideas of reason and choice, both individual and social, that are now taken for granted in economic theory (and also in certain kinds of political theory) clearly reflects a distinct image of what human beings are assumed to be: they are essentially self-interested individuals who, by making rational choices, seek to achieve the greatest possible satisfaction and advantage by 'maximizing' their preferences or, in non-theoretical terms, by getting what they want. Of course, young people usually go through a period of rebellion and non-conformity, but ultimately individuals fall into patterns of life, work and leisure for which they have been prepared by parenting, education and the culture they both absorb and sustain. They come to value success in competitive environments and enjoy the rewards that such success can bring for themselves and their families. Given the widespread loss of community, brought about in part by the mentality fostered by economic competitiveness, by long hours of work (the 'workaholic' is one of the heroes of our society), and the time which individuals spend pursuing various kinds of entertainment, human lives are more 'individualistic', less 'communal', and less committed to the tasks and responsibilities of good citizenship than they might be and, ideally, should be. Politicians may from time to time catch glimpses of this and express their regret, but they can do little to alter it, principally because they are unable to understand that the economic system and ethos they support are among the primary causes of the destruction they lament.

But at a deeper level large numbers of people would seem to have accepted a particular 'philosophical' idea of human nature, a materialist and wholly secular view of what they are. Plato might have noted that they also seem to have accepted a sense of morality that, although frequently outraged by instances of evil, iniquity and scandal, is not seriously devoted to ideals of virtue and justice, more concerned with conformity or aspiration and conduct – the acquisition of property, the pursuit of personal happiness and the enjoyment of leisure – than with ethical and political concerns. Plato broke away from the naturalism of the early philosophers because it could not, in his view, do justice to the uniqueness of the mental life of human beings and the moral status of the human soul. Today, a naturalist philosophy, based on the principle that human beings are entirely physical creatures whose behaviour can be explained, like everything else in nature, by science, seems to have encouraged the belief that only 'material' value, particularly the pursuit of wealth, status and celebrity, can give meaning to human lives.

This 'picture' is, of course, too simple. Our society is complex and human life within it far more varied and culturally diverse than in Plato's Athens. What Plato is likely to have observed are widespread tendencies and trends rather than permanent and universal features of our society. Nevertheless, such phenomena are worth noting and Plato would have encouraged us to question whether the naturalist-materialist theory of human nature is completely convincing. Perhaps patient and critical reflection will reveal that the theory, in spite of widespread acceptance, is not entirely coherent and compelling. In particular, Plato may well have asked us to consider whether we might be able to aspire to a 'higher' vision of what would give real value and meaning to our lives, taking our inspiration from those who act with great courage and a sense of duty and sacrifice at times of disaster and crisis as well as those who, both in private and public life, behave with integrity, dignity and honour.

Plato did not believe in, and might not have been able to understand, progress in the modern sense, but neither did he encourage people simply to accept and comply with the changes that occurred in the world around them. He was sufficiently optimistic to believe that human improvement was possible, both in the character of individual lives and that of society, and in the possibility of achieving freedom from the forces that distort personal development and undermine their capacity for virtue and happiness. It is probable that Plato would have suggested that we still have much to reflect about and understand.

▶ Democracy

It is likely that our time-travelling Plato would have been intensely interested in the current state of our representative democracy in comparison with the Athenian model that, along with tyranny, oligarchy and military rule, he condemned as unjust. We can guess that he would have picked out accountability as a central principle of representative democracy, the relationship between modern democracy and justice, the role and power of political parties, the character and education of parliamentary members, and the ideas and purposes that inform political policies and practices as topics of special concern.

He might well have begun his review by reminding us that our democracy, just like the Athenian system, was not in itself a guarantee of justice. A democracy has more to do with procedures and practices of election, the practice of policy making and the rules of legislation than with a substantial idea of justice: a democracy, whether direct or representative, is perfectly capable of establishing a government whose policies are morally reprehensible, socially divisive, and economically destructive. Plato's point would be that an acceptable democracy must be informed by the principles of justice in order to promote the happiness of everyone in a society. The crucial question that Athenian democracy needed to address was precisely the same as the question we still face today, that of what justice really is, a question which concerns the relationship between authority and power as well as the fundamental ideas of freedom and equality. In a representative democracy a government derives its authority from the people who elect it to office and in this connection Plato might well have observed that those in government, once elected, break many of the promises that helped secure their election as well as introducing policies that had not been mentioned in their electoral campaign. He might also have observed that once a party has been elected, it seeks to remain in power for as long as possible, irrespective of whether its work in government has been successful, to win further elections and, in theory at least, to remain in power forever more. Both observations, he might have said, are indicative of one of the most common shortcomings of representative democracies: a lack of integrity on the part of politicians and parties combined with a lack of respect for the individual citizens who voted for them in good faith, features of the system which make governments less accountable than they ought to be. This can have unfortunate consequences: the dwindling number of citizens who cast their votes in parliamentary elections and who take part in political debate suggests that the electorate has indeed lost respect for politicians and the parties they belong to, a situation which undermines the health, and perhaps the very existence, of a democracy.

According to Plato a just society will promote the happiness of all citizens by bringing about social harmony and unity. In this connection Plato might well have drawn attention to the way in which a system of government, based on the role and activity of political parties staffed by professional politicians, officials and activists, reflects division and disunity in society: this undermines the possibility of real justice simply because of the tendency within the system to allow political policy and legislation to be determined by what Thrasymachus, at the beginning of the *Republic*, called 'the advantage of the stronger party' (*Republic* 338c) rather by what is of advantage to the people as a whole.

In one of his very late works, the *Laws*, the character called The Athenian, in the context of discussing retail trade, states: 'When goods of any kind are distributed disproportionately and unequally, anyone who makes the distribution equal and even cannot fail to do good' (*Laws* 918b). Plato would surely have judged us unfavourably for allowing inequality (of wealth, status and power) to become such a prominent feature of our society, for resigning ourselves to unacceptable levels of poverty, unemployment and crime, to significant variations in the provision of adequate education, and for abandoning considerable numbers of individuals as posing an intractable problem rather than seeing them as fellow citizens who have become victims of injustice and a morally indifferent economic order.

We can now state the main reason why Plato would have expressed these views. There is a fundamental assumption at work in Plato's inquiry into justice in the *Republic*, one that applies to all political states entitled to be called just: those in political authority must be able to view the society they govern from the right perspective, the perspective demanded by the very idea of justice. Plato exploits the whole idea of guardianship to make this point. The Guardians, although citizens, are not fully within the life of the society they govern and, therefore, do not identify with any social group or sector that would seek to further the advantage of its members at the expense of others; the Guardians are to govern from the independent and impartial perspective of what would now be called the State, the system of authority, based on knowledge and wisdom, which is to protect the rights of all citizens, promote their well-being and happiness, and ensure their safety and security. If the politicians and parties that hold office in a democracy, whether direct or representative, become too closely tied to the interests of social classes, private commercial interests, and the interests of the financial and banking sectors of the economy (all of them quite obvious features of British society), the perspective of justice – perhaps we should say the perspective of *real* justice – will have been abandoned. The same consideration would also apply to the relationship between government and media, generally referred to as 'the media', in a liberal democracy, a system of government that may vary considerably in its commitment to both liberal and democratic principles. We can be certain that Plato would have been critical of any form of State in which political integrity and a commitment to justice had been compromised by the subservience of politicians to the power of the media. Plato, of course, would have denied the media any place in his vision of a just society, but he might also have acknowledged the important function of intelligent and morally responsible forms of communication through media in a liberal democracy while deploring our failure to ensure that the media conform to the highest standards of truth and decency. He would challenge us to make sure that these standards are met.

Our discussion of the perspective of justice in relation to modern representative democracy should call to mind that Plato was as concerned with understanding injustice as he was with uncovering what real justice actually involved. He was in his own time familiar with the type of oligarchic State in which wealth is the principal, indeed the only, standard of value and, unsurprisingly, what qualifies particular individuals for political rule. Plato might well have said that our democracy in some of its recent phases comes closer to resembling an oligarchy than a democracy in which politicians are devoted to the task of maintaining real justice.

Finally, now that we are aware of Plato's view on the qualifications and the preparations of individuals for the role of guardianship, an obvious comment: Plato would surely have raised the question of whether our politicians are properly educated for the task of ruling a just society. This is not a negligible matter. It is not that that most politicians have not been educated in the 'conventional' sense but rather of their inability to derive from their education the depth of knowledge, understanding and moral integrity that are essential requirements of good government.

▶ Education

In the just society that Socrates and his companions work out in the *Republic*, education will be made compulsory by the State, its content will be determined by the Guardians and it will be carefully supervised either by the Guardians themselves or by properly qualified delegates. Education is far too important in relation to justice and citizenship to be left to what would now be called 'the private sector', to families and to privately paid teachers such as the Sophists.

Education in the United Kingdom has changed considerably since the end of the Second World War. There is now a widespread belief that education should be primarily a matter of gaining qualifications that are ultimately connected with the economy, that it is concerned with the skills required in industrial production (although manufacturing industries have declined dramatically since the early 1980s), the 'communication industries', the 'leisure industry', the financial and banking sector of the economy, and so forth: simply put, it is widely assumed that what goes on in educational environments should reflect what is called 'the world of work'. One of the interesting consequences of the movement towards vocational forms of schooling and training is that the expression 'a liberal education' has virtually disappeared from the vocabulary of teachers and educational theorists and with it the idea that the *ultimate* aim of education is to liberate, to free individual persons from ignorance, from any form of belief that would stunt and distort the intellectual and moral development which prepare individuals to become free and responsible citizens whose lives would have been enriched through education.

However, linking education with skills, employment and the needs of the economy has not solved the problem of what the real aims of education ought to be; it has actually made it more acute. It is true that one of the most important tasks of government in a liberal democracy is to ensure that young people are given an appropriate education. It is also true that successive governments during the last 50 years have attached great importance to educational policy and have, from time to time, made rather dramatic (if rather hollow) pronouncements regarding their commitment: 'Education, Education, Education'. And yet, what Plato is likely to have observed is confusion and uncertainty over the content and purpose of education. In a public culture dominated by market considerations value is inevitably transferred from objects that interest and attract people to their monetary value, a process which eventually leads to an inability to evaluate and appreciate things for what they are in themselves and for their own sake. This has been allowed to happen and even encouraged in the field of education. School education remains a public service paid for by revenue from taxation, but it has become increasingly viewed as open to commercial sponsorship and influence. And higher education is now regarded as a financial investment for personal advantage on the part of students who incur considerable debt in order to pay for the courses they follow in colleges and universities. For Plato this would have been a dangerous development.

Education is ultimately the moral and cultural education of citizens whose lives will make a positive contribution to sustaining a just society: this is the responsibility of the State, not a matter for commercial investment. Plato might have suggested that we would do well to retrieve the idea that the real value of education lies both in its contribution to the quality of individual life and to the moral and cultural ethos of a just society.

Given Plato's abiding interest in media and its consequences in society, we should give him the last word here. During his period of observation he will have noticed a major change taking place in the various settings in which education is conducted, a move away from the reading and study of books and towards the 'texts' that are placed on the screens of computers and tablets. Such a change may seem attractive and progressive because they are technologically impressive and superficially exciting: like all technological innovations and advances what they promise for the future is irresistible. It is, I think, certain that Plato would have advised us to view this development with great caution, to think very carefully about what the consequences of such a change might be. Here we are, in the twenty-first century, over 2,000 years since Plato's life and work; perhaps only he could have fully grasped the irony of the obvious question: could it be that the education young people now receive is actually hastening their return to the Cave rather than keeping them out of it?

▶ Public culture

Before we consider Plato's likely reflections on the current state of art in our society, we will look briefly at what might have interested Plato about the nature and quality of our public culture. It would have been quite obvious to him that our public culture is dominated by forms of entertainment provided largely through the technology of the screen. Live entertainment remains available, of course, particularly in the areas of music, theatre and sport, but the screen has become so dominant that we can easily imagine Plato believing that we have returned to the world of the Cave, the situation in which our sensibility, values, tastes and desires are decisively shaped by what we absorb from the images presented to us. We have already considered the power of media in connection with politics; we will now look at the role of media in public culture.

What Plato is most likely to have identified as a mater of serious concern are the twin problems of media quantity and media quality. There are just so many kinds of media, so many television channels, so many programmes of so many different kinds, so many computer programmes and games, and so forth, that describing our society as 'media saturated' seems obviously appropriate. But is this state of affairs actually desirable? Do the media that pervade our culture really contribute to human well-being and happiness, both of which, for Plato, depend on freedom from the control and manipulation that the use of media can inflict on us? The technologies of the screen and the images and texts that pass across them have become so influential, in our work as well as our leisure, that it is worth questioning whether this phenomenon is genuinely beneficial, whether the effect of a screen-dominated culture is a distraction from reality rather than a force for liberation. The image of the Cave represented an imprisonment or enslavement by ignorance, illusion, ephemeral interests and harmful desires, from which only the truth can free us: surely Plato's verdict on our screen-dominated culture would have been severely critical.

But there is the further problem of cultural quality. What we view on our screens is, to say the least, of variable quality: endless 'soap operas', dramas involving crime and violence, so-called 'reality' television shows, undemanding quiz programmes, features on various forms of human deformity that are reminiscent of the 'freak shows' of the fairgrounds of the past – how little our interests and tastes seem to have improved! Could it be that our media-dominated culture is such that its effect is exactly the same as that of the Cave, *not* to stimulate intelligence, to increase understanding, to cultivate good taste, and to 'humanize' personal lives, but to distract individuals into an unthinking acceptance of their captivity. Plato's challenge would be to ask whether his image of the Cave conveys the real nature of our public culture in the way that he thought it did of the Athenian society of his time. If it does, then we should consider what may be done to liberate ourselves from this condition.

▶ Art

In 1994 the artist Damien Hirst exhibited his creation 'Away From the Flock', a dead sheep immersed in a glass tank filled with formaldehyde, a work that anticipated a later work by the same artist consisting of a dead shark similarly suspended and named 'The Physical Impossibility of Death in the Mind of Someone Living'. In 2007 Hirst created a work called 'For the Love of God', a platinum cast of a human skull encrusted with diamonds. This work has been said to have cost 14 million pounds to make and to have been sold for around 50 million pounds, a considerable return on the original investment. In the 1990s the artist Tracey Emin became famous for her work entitled 'My Bed' (unmade) and a creation which consisted of a tent on which was written the names of everyone Emin had ever slept with. In 2001 the artist Martin Creed won the Turner Prize, an annual award for interesting and challenging contemporary art, with a work called 'Work no. 227; the lights going on and off', which consisted of a small artificial room in which lights did indeed go on and off.

▲ The Tate Modern gallery

It is not easy to know what to make of such creations. They attract considerable attention and the artists who create them are well known and even become celebrities; some of these works are bought and sold for large sums of money and for some – directors of art galleries and critics, for example – they seem to have interest and value. For others, such as the art critic Robert Hughes, these creations are largely devoid of genuine merit and are to be condemned as the products of clever charlatans who have been able to exploit the dubious taste of patrons and collectors.

How would Plato have responded to such art? It is, I think, more than likely that he would have found it interesting, not because of the real artistic value of particular works but because of what it reveals about our contemporary culture. He might well have formed the view that such creations differ significantly from works of art that have in the past aimed at certain kinds of 'truth', for example the truth about persons in portraiture, the might of a nation in scenes of military victory, the rich beauty of national landscapes, and the energy and fervour of a revolutionary movement. Such works are created with great skill and craftsmanship and express the visions of particular artists. Many works of conceptual art and items of installation are, on the other hand, in harmony with some of the most notable features of contemporary culture and entertainment, a taste for what is novel and shocking without being arresting, interesting and disturbing in the way traditional forms of art – in literature, visual arts and music – generally are. Plato might well have suggested that we should look at contemporary forms of art in the context of a wider public culture dominated, even overwhelmed, by the shallowness of fame, glamour and celebrity that rarely derive from genuine talent and achievement. Is this the shallow art of a shallow culture? Given that Plato relentlessly championed the principle that we should *know* what is good for us rather than allow the forces of persuasion to determine what that should be, this is likely to have been his challenge.

I would also suggest that Plato would have spotted how the kind of contemporary art we are considering is very much in harmony with the economic ethos of our time, a social 'atmosphere' in which market value can often seem to be the only kind of value that is understood and respected. Such art is symptomatic of the limits of our contemporary sensibility, a taste for what is novel, sensational and ephemeral, an art of appearance rather than reality, and even of cynical manipulation, rather than the moral and artistic depth that aims at the truthful comprehension of human life, society and ultimately of the world of which we are a part.

But is such art a cause for concern? Plato, as we have noted, did take art to be a matter of serious interest and concern: art can be a force for harm in a just society; the power of art is the power of the image and, therefore, comparable to the power of oratory to persuade and influence in the absence of real knowledge and understanding. For Plato bad art is harmful for both individuals and society, a distraction from what is of real value, but good art can be even worse, far more powerful, and, therefore, far more damaging. This is a paradox in Plato's discussion of art that we would do well to contemplate. The art that is characteristic of our contemporary culture may well be of negligible value as art; the crucial issue is what it reveals to us about ourselves and the social and cultural ethos that, like a wild garden that we never planned, has grown around us.

And this, of course, is the challenge that we have extended to Plato's philosophy as a whole, one that requires us to either defend or criticize what we think we know, what we think is valuable, what we aspire to achieve.

Appendix: Plato and modern ideologies

The society constructed in Plato's *Republic* would seem on the surface to be remarkably similar to very many of the historical and contemporary societies we are familiar with. Such societies resemble the republic in that the tasks of government are in the hands of a small number of individual persons who have, in one way or another, acquired this role, maintaining the external security and internal order of the society is entrusted to suitably qualified and trained personnel and, finally, the economic life of the society as a whole is sustained by producers, traders and merchants who have a flair for such work. What makes the republic distinctive is that the individuals who belong to the ruling group are qualified and selected for office by their intelligence, virtue and education; they do not acquire authority by virtue of aristocratic birth, the economic power of the class they belong to, or by democratic election. However, the fact that Plato ruled out democracy as a means of choosing political leaders has led some of his critics to accuse him of defending a reprehensible political ideology rather than conducting a genuinely philosophical inquiry into the nature of justice. Richard Crossman, in his book *Plato Today* (first published in 1937 during the European crisis that was to lead to the Second World War) portrayed Plato as an early fascist who would have approved of at least some aspects of Nazi Germany under Hitler. Karl Popper, in his famous book *The Open Society and its Enemies*, which appeared in 1945, accused Plato of defending an early example of a totalitarian ideology, a political system by which the State, as in the Soviet Union under Joseph Stalin, seeks to exercise complete control over every aspect of personal, social and cultural life. I believe that such claims are misguided and distort the real nature and value of Plato's inquiry.

Political ideologies are very much a feature of modern European societies. Systems of political beliefs and purposes, such as liberalism, conservatism, socialism, communism and fascism, came to prominence during the eighteenth and nineteenth centuries and gradually came to express the ideals and aims of political parties, an aspect of modern politics that was completely absent from Plato's Athens. What, then, is an ideology? All ideologies consist of ideas and purposes that must, I think, be understood in political terms. Here we will follow Andrew Heywood's definition of an ideology:

An ideology is a more or less coherent set of ideas that provides that basis for organized political action, whether this is intended to preserve, modify or overthrow the existing system of power. All ideologies therefore (a) offer an account of the existing order, usually in the form of a 'world-view', (b) advance a model of a desired future, a vision of the 'good society', and (c) explain how political change can and should be brought about – how to get from (a) to (b).

Andrew Heywood, Political Ideologies
(Palgrave Macmillan, 1992) p.12.

This definition clearly implies that an ideology is very different from the character and purpose of a scientific theory. The function of a scientific theory is to explain a particular aspect of nature, the motion of objects, for example, and it is accepted as true if it can be confirmed by experimental results. The aim of a scientific theory, like the aim of science in general, is to make sense of the world objectively, the world as it really is rather than as we want it to be, from which it follows that a scientific theory will be modified or even completely abandoned if experimental results make this necessary. The function of an ideology is quite different, not that of explaining features of nature but rather, as Heywood's definition implies, to justify a particular view of how society ought to be structured and ruled. Unlike the content of a scientific theory, which will consist of concepts and principles selected to comprehend a particular aspect of nature, those who form and promote an ideology will make use of ideas, beliefs, and even prejudices, purely because they further the interests and ambitions of those who are represented by a political party or movement. From the perspective of Plato's philosophy, the function of a modern ideology is to persuade, to produce conviction and commitment rather than to communicate truth, knowledge and the reality of justice. In this sense the role of an ideology may be connected with the argument advanced by Thrasymachus at the beginning of *Republic*, namely that since ideas of justice invariably reflect the interests of the strongest group in society there can be no such thing as real justice. However, an ideology may also express the political ambitions of a disadvantaged social group, even to the point of inspiring revolutionary action. In order to fully clarify the difference between ideology and philosophy it is important to look carefully at what may be called the content of ideologies.

Although there are now a number of particular ideologies devoted to limited political causes – nationalism, feminism and environmentalism are clear examples – we will confine our attention to the five most comprehensive ideologies that have dominated modern politics: fascism, conservatism, liberalism, socialism and communism. The worldviews that form a part of the content of these ideologies typically include, (a) a moral theory concerning the concepts of freedom and equality centred on the question of how much freedom individuals should enjoy in relation to the State, and (b) a theory concerning the nature of human beings and how they develop in relation to their environment and education. In brief, an ideology will tend to endorse either a libertarian or collectivist view of individual freedom and equality in society, the former being the principle that individual persons should enjoy the maximum degree of freedom to shape their lives in the way they want to, the latter being the principle that a political State is justified in limiting individual freedom in certain respects in order to bring about greater equality and security. As Plato fully recognized, some individuals are stronger and cleverer than others and are likely to further their own advantage at the expense of their fellow citizens: in this connection the idea of justice identified and clarified by Plato leans towards collectivism rather than unqualified libertarianism. Quite clearly, liberalism and certain versions of conservatism endorse libertarianism while socialism and communism generally favour collectivist policies and practices. With regard to human nature and human development, one theory insists that children and young people should be given the maximum degree of freedom in family and educational settings in order to allow the natural and healthy development of their unique individual potential while the opposing theory denies the existence of natural potential and advocates moulding and shaping young persons to fit the kind of society an ideology is intended to justify. Once again we can see how an emphasis on free development is likely to fit into a liberal ideology while a more restrictive and disciplined view of child-rearing and education is more likely to find a place in socialist and communist ideologies. However, these assumptions would be over hasty. In the liberal democracy of the United States, for example, education includes policies and practices that are designed to induce a strong commitment to the American nation and the values that define it while many defenders of socialism reject the assumption that both a socialist state and its social and educational ethos must be authoritarian in character. What we learn from these observations, however, is that ideologies tend to include and combine ideas and assumptions in order to further political purposes rather than subjecting them to critical and evaluative scrutiny, in order to persuade rather than to enlighten and educate. The purpose of philosophy, and indeed the sciences, arts and humanities in general, is not to persuade but to pursue the kind of objective, critical and evaluative study that is central to education. This is why the data obtained by scientific investigation and the scrutiny of concepts and arguments by philosophers are often unwelcome to, and often ignored by, politicians whose policies, decisions and actions are shaped by the ideology of their party rather than by the truth.

It will be clear from what has been said in this book that Plato, in company with many philosophers in the long history of the subject, was indeed concerned with freedom and equality, with the nature of persons, and with the kind of education that should be provided for the young in society. What makes his inquiry into these topics distinctively philosophical is its devotion to clarifying the reality of such matters rather than a concern with purposes determined by the interests of social classes and the strategies of political parties.

10 great works by Plato

1. *Defence of Socrates* tr. David Gallop (Oxford World's Classics, 2008), also known as the *Apology*, this is Plato's version of Socrates' speech at his trial.

2. *Phaedo* tr. G. M. A. Grube (Hackett Publishing Company, 1977), a brilliant dialogue on the soul and the possibility of life after death; it also introduces the theory of Forms or ideas.

3. *Gorgias* tr. Robin Waterfield (Oxford World's Classics, 1994), an important early dialogue on language, oratory and the ethical views of Socrates.

4. *Protagoras* tr. C. C. W. Taylor (Oxford World's Classics, 2009), a fascinating work featuring the famous Sophist, Protagoras, on virtue and knowledge and on whether virtue can be taught.

5. *Meno* tr. Robin Waterfield (Oxford World's Classics, 2009), an interesting dialogue which throws light on the development of Plato's views on knowledge.

6. *Republic* tr. Robin Waterfield (Oxford World's Classics, 2008), one of the greatest works of philosophy and one of the great books of the world, it covers a wide range of topics, most importantly those of justice, virtue, knowledge, the soul, citizenship, education and art.

7. *Phaedrus* tr. Robin Waterfield (Oxford World's Classics, 2009), an important work in which the soul is explained by the image of a charioteer (reason) seeking to control two unruly horses, a white horse (spirit) and a black horse (desire). The dialogue also discusses love and characterizes obsessive love as a form of madness.

8. *Theaetetus* tr. John McDowell (Oxford University Press, 1985), an important work on knowledge containing Plato's arguments against Protagoras' relativism.

9. *Sophist* tr. Nicholas P. White (Hackett Publishing Company, 1997), a difficult but crucially important work on language containing Plato's account of meaning and truth and the relationship between language and the world.

10. *Laws* tr. T. J. Saunders (Penguin Classics, 1970), a late work on politics, more of a practical manual than the *Republic*, it is exceptionally interesting on topics such as law, administration, education, religion and the economy.

10 important Greek philosophical words

11. *phusis*: an important word translated to mean 'nature', the nature or essence of something, the natural world, nature in contrast to convention.

12. *logos*: one of the most important words in the Greek philosophical vocabulary, translated as 'to speak' or 'to say something'; it was also used to mean 'reason', 'account' (explanation, formula and definition); the word is also connected with the idea of argument, *logicos*.

13. *psukhe*: translated as 'soul' and associated with the idea of life and, in Plato, the possibility of immortality.

14. *gnosis*: translated as 'knowledge' and 'knowable'; knowledge of Forms or ideas which is different from beliefs or opinions arising from experiences and desires.

15. *doxa*: translated as 'opinion', belief that does not meet the standards governing knowledge.

16. *eidos*: translated as Form or idea; the Form or idea *of* something; what something really or essentially is; shape,

that of a cube, for example, is the visible appearance of a Form, but the Form itself is not visible.

17. *ethos*: translated as 'habit', 'custom', 'way of life'; close to the idea of culture.

18. *arete*: translated as 'goodness', 'excellence', and, after the Latin *virtus*, as 'virtue'.

19. *dikaiosune*: translated as 'justice', to 'act justly', e.g. fairly, honestly, decently; in the *Phaedo* justice is associated with harmony or attunement in the soul.

20. *dialektike*: translated as 'dialectic', meaning in Plato a logically structured conversation aimed at uncovering falsehood and confusion and revealing what is meaningful and true. For Plato, dialectic, unlike the techniques of persuasion employed by the Sophists, is the method of philosophy.

10 books on Plato's philosophy

21. David Evans, *A Plato Primer* (Acumen, 2010), a very good introductory book on the major philosophical topics discussed by Plato.

22. Andrew S. Mason, *Plato* (Acumen, 2010), a clear and readable survey of Plato's work.

23. Hugh H. Benson (ed.), *A Companion to Plato* (Blackwell, 2009), an excellent collection of readable articles on every aspect of Plato's philosophy.

24. Richard Kraut (ed.), *The Cambridge Companion to Plato* (Cambridge University Press, 1992), a valuable collection of essays on major themes in Plato's work.

25. Malcolm Schofield, *Plato: Political Philosophy* (Oxford University Press, 2006), an excellent book on Plato's political philosophy, particularly good on topics covered in this book such as money, education and citizenship.

26. Julia Annas, *An Introduction to Plato's* Republic (Oxford University Press, 1981), an excellent book on Plato's most famous work.

27. Nickolas Pappas, *Plato and the Republic* (Routledge, 1995), a detailed and useful guide to the main ideas and arguments in the *Republic*.

28. Karl R. Popper, *The Open Society and its Enemies,* vol. 1, *The Spell of Plato* (One Volume Edition, Princeton University Press, 2013), a famous and controversial work that is highly critical of Plato: Popper interprets Plato as a precursor of modern totalitarianism.

29. Simon Blackburn, *Plato's* Republic (Atlantic Books, 2006), a readable and lively but highly critical reading of the *Republic*.

30. Melissa Lane, *Plato's Progeny* (Duckworth, 2001), a fascinating book on the different ways Plato's philosophy has been interpreted in different societies in different historical eras. Plato's popularity in nineteenth-century England is particularly interesting.

10 books on the ancient Greek world

31. Robin and Kathryn Waterfield, *The Greek Myths* (Quercus, 2011), an excellent re-telling of the myths through which the Greeks understood themselves and the world before philosophy and science.

32. Robin Waterfield (ed. and tr.), *The First Philosophers; the Presocratics and the Sophists* (Oxford World's Classics, 2009), a comprehensive and clear translation of early Greek philosophical texts including Thales, Anaximander, Heraclitus, Parmenides and Gorgias.

33. Julia Annas, *Ancient Philosophy: a Very Short Introduction* (Oxford University Press, 2000), a very good introduction the major developments and topics in Greek philosophy.

34. John Boardman, Jasper Griffin and Oswyn Murray, *The Oxford Illustrated History of Greece and the Hellenistic World* (Oxford University Press, 2001), a very good and well-illustrated history of the Greek world that forms the background to Plato's philosophy.

35. Pierre Leveque, *Ancient Greece: Utopia and Reality* (Thames and Hudson, 1990), a readable and very well-illustrated account of the world of Ancient Greece, it also includes a selection of useful documents.

36. Paul Cartledge, *Ancient Greece: a Very Short Introduction* (Oxford University Press, 2011), a valuable survey of the Greek world concentrating on the most important cities.

37. John Boardman, *Greek Art* (Thames and Hudson, 1996), a very good book on all aspects of Greek art.

38. Sitta von Redden, *Money in Classical Antiquity* (Cambridge University Press, 2012), an indispensable book on the background to Plato's interest in money.

39. Paul Cartledge, *Ancient Greek Political Thought in Practice* (Cambridge University Press, 2009), a valuable book on the variety of political systems in the ancient Greek world which includes a chapter on the trial of Socrates and another chapter on ancient and modern democracy.

40. Simon Hornblower and Antony Spawforth (eds.), *The Oxford Companion to Classical Civilization* (Oxford University Press, 1998), an extremely valuable book on all aspects of Greek history and culture, including philosophy, literature, religion, art, politics and war.

10 films and documentaries on themes in Plato's philosophy

41. *Double Indemnity*, dir. Billy Wilder, 1944: a classic film noir; revealing on Plato's early theory of the human soul.

42. *Vertigo*, dir. Alfred Hitchcock, 1959: a masterpiece on the themes of appearance and reality and the consequences of obsessive love.

43. *Wall Street*, dir. Oliver Stone, 1998: a film on the deregulated financial world of the 1980s that led to the crisis of 2008; famous for introducing the expression, 'greed is good'.

44. *The Colour of Money*, dir. Martin Scorsese, 1987: an excellent film, like its predecessor, Robert Rossen's *The Hustler*, on the conflict between the motive of financial gain and personal integrity.

45. *Summer and Smoke*, dir. Peter Glenville, 1961: based on a play by Tennessee Williams, an interesting film on the religious idea of the soul that originated with Plato.

46. *Woman of the Year*, dir. George Stevens, 1942: a fine Hollywood comedy on the theme of gender equality in the workplace.

47. *It's a Wonderful Life*, dir. Frank Capra, 1947: a wonderful film which involves almost every philosophical question discussed by Plato; a classic defence of liberalism against the background of President Roosevelt's response to the Great Depression known as the New Deal.

48. *Enemy of the State*, dir. Tony Scott, 1998: an exciting film on the way in which electronic surveillance through screen technology threatens personal freedom in a liberal democracy.

49. *Inside Job*, dir. Charles Ferguson, 2011: an excellent documentary on the causes and consequences of the financial crisis of 2008.

50. *The Trap: What Happened to Our Dream of Freedom?* dir. Adam Curtis, 2007: a brilliant and disturbing series of three documentaries on the idea of freedom in the contemporary world. The first is particularly good on the idea of the person employed in economic theory, the third

is a fascinating inquiry into ideas of freedom in the world following the end of the Cold War.

10 books on two themes in Plato's philosophy: money and art

51. Joseph Stiglitz, *Freefall: free markets and the sinking of the global economy* (Penguin Books, 2010), an excellent inquiry into the financial crash of 2008 written by a distinguished economist.

52. Robert Harris, *The Fear Index* (Hutchinson, 2011), a good and disturbing novel on the use of computer programmes in the field of financial investment.

53. David Harvey, *A Brief History of Neoliberalism* (Oxford University Press, 2005), an important discussion of neoliberal economic and political thinking and its influence on contemporary politics.

54. Robert Skidelski and Edward Skidelski, *How Much is Enough? The Love of Money and the Good Life* (Allen Lane, 2012), a challenging discussion of wealth and the quality of life that echoes Plato's interest in money.

55. Michael Sandel, *What Money Can't Buy: the Moral Limits of Markets* (Allen Lane, 2012), a lively inquiry into the dominance of money and market values by a distinguished contemporary philosopher.

56. David Cottington, *Modern Art: a Very Short Introduction* (Oxford University Press, 2005), a good survey of developments in art in the twentieth and twenty-first centuries.

57. Cynthia Freedland, *But is it Art?* (Oxford University Press, 2001), an interesting discussion of contemporary art from the perspective of art theory.

58. Matthew Collings, *This is Modern Art* (Weidenfeld and Nicholson, 1999), a lively and well-illustrated book on major trends and artists in the modern and contemporary periods.

59. Julian Stallybrass, *High Art Life: the Rise and Fall of British Art* (Verso, 2006), an interesting book on contemporary British art.

60. Robert Hughes, *The Shock of the New* (Thames and Hudson, 1991), a well-known critical book on the development of modern art by a famous art critic.

10 negative questions concerning Plato's political philosophy

61. **The authoritarian temptation:** it has always been tempting to read Plato as defending a form of authoritarian, even totalitarian, state. Can this temptation be resisted?

62. **The threat of censorship:** we value freedom of speech, but we also recognize that this freedom can be abused. How important is freedom of speech? What are its limits?

63. **A concern over indoctrination:** Plato attached great importance to education, particularly in relation to citizenship; in authoritarian regimes, education has always involved methods of indoctrination by which individuals are made to believe things without reason, but in a liberal democracy indoctrination is morally unacceptable. Can indoctrination be avoided?

64. **A worry over social rigidity:** the *Republic* seems to present a highly ordered and rigidly stratified society, whereas social mobility and social status by personal achievement are prominent features of liberal democracies. How far should social rigidity be a matter of concern?

65. **The possibility of insularity:** the *Republic* can suggest a rather inward-looking community, concerned with its own internal order, its way of life and military strength against the threat of external attack. It is important to consider whether insularity and a reluctance to enter into co-operative relations with other states and societies are actually desirable.

66. **A concern over the importance of the family as a social institution:** it is widely believed that Plato took a very negative view of the family and its role in a just society. Is the family really an obstacle to social justice and stability?

67. **Lack of creativity:** it is widely assumed that artistic creativity can only flourish in a free society (which is not strictly true: the music of Dmitri Shostakovich in the Soviet Union is an obvious example). Is the idea of a just society as Plato imagines it really an obstacle to real artistic creativity and to enriching a society's culture?

68. **Loss of initiative:** there is a similar worry concerning individual initiative and enterprise, generally regarded as valuable personal qualities in a thriving society. Might it not be that Plato's just state would encourage conformity and passivity rather than individual drive and achievement?

69. **Poverty:** Plato insisted that the economic life of a just society must be closely and carefully regulated. Would this mean that the level of individual income and general prosperity in such a society would be relatively low? Is a lower standard of living a 'price' worth paying for justice?

70. **Individuality and Identity:** in a liberal democracy a sense of individuality and a strong sense of individual identity are encouraged. Could it be that Plato's emphasis on regulation and social order and harmony would actually undermine individuality and weaken individual identity while encouraging persons to identify themselves more

with their community, as in a tribe or a traditional community, rather than as autonomous selves?

10 positive reminders from Plato's philosophy

71. **Justice:** has justice become the forgotten ideal? Plato's great interest in the idea of justice and how it should be realized in practice should remind us to give serious thought to the value of justice in human life.

72. **Equality:** this idea is fundamentally connected with justice: what do we mean by equality? Why is equality important? These are questions that require serious consideration.

73. **Virtue:** in our concern for a good life, defined in terms of prosperity, success and pleasure, have we forgotten what is of the greatest importance for the quality of life? Plato reminds us that this is virtue, a virtuous character expressed in virtuous behaviour,

74. **Freedom:** for Plato freedom was as important as equality, but how should this idea be understood? In a liberal society freedom is a matter of intention and action, of being able to do what we want without restraint or interference. For Plato, however, freedom was more a matter of being free from causal influences that would undermine our virtue and happiness, which was not, he believed, incompatible with there being logical constraints that make knowledge, communication, virtue and justice what they are. The nature and limits of freedom is a matter for serious inquiry.

75. **Good government:** Plato emphasized the importance of good government by intelligent, properly educated and wise politicians. His contribution to political philosophy should remind us that this is a matter for serious discussion.

76. **Education:** the degree of importance Plato attached to education should prompt us to think hard about what the real nature and purpose of education should be. Plato's work should remind us that there are important relationships between education and the moral development of persons that lays the foundations of good citizenship.

77. **Citizenship:** citizenship has a number of important aspects: it is a relationship of status between an individual and a state, usually determined by birth or naturalization (in Athens only children born of Athenians were automatically granted citizenship, but there were exceptions: the great banker Pasion, for example, was originally a slave but he had been able to buy his citizenship); but citizenship is also a moral ideal in that a person is expected to meet certain obligations as a *good* citizen; citizenship can also be a matter of identity in that, in some societies, a person is expected to be, for example, both a citizen of Athens and Athenian as a matter of identity. Plato's concern with citizenship is a topic for serious discussion.

78. **Entertainment and culture:** Plato placed reality above appearance, and knowledge of what is real is the key to the good life. Entertainment and culture in general should, for Plato, be of the highest quality; standards of quality, in craftsmanship and architecture, for example, should reflect what is of value and importance for human beings. We should think carefully about standards of quality in relation to forms of entertainment and culture.

79. **Knowledge:** knowledge, which derives ultimately from rational thought, is, Plato claims, of the highest importance. We value scientific knowledge, particularly its application in technology and fields of practice such as medicine and agriculture. But we have also become infatuated with information because of its practical value and the ease with which it can be obtained and applied through computer technology. Plato's inquiries into truth,

knowledge and communication should inspire us to think hard about the real nature of knowledge and what forms of knowledge are important to us.

80. **Art:** finally art. Plato was suspicious of art and of artists; his interest in this field should remind us that art is not a trivial matter, that art can be important and a topic for serious thought.

10 modern philosophers and their works

81. **Rene Descartes (1595–1650):** generally referred to as the father of modern philosophy, Descartes was a rationalist (certain knowledge is the result of reasoning rather than sense experience) and the first modern defender of dualism (a person is composed of two different substances, mind and body). He also shared Plato's conviction that the world was rationally ordered. His most famous work is *Meditations on First Philosophy* (in *Descartes: Selected Philosophical Writings*, tr. John Cottingham, Robert Stoothoff and Dugald Murdoch (Cambridge University Press, 1985)).

82. **Thomas Hobbes (1588–1679):** Hobbes followed Plato in basing his political philosophy on a philosophical understanding of the world (he was a materialist) and human nature (he believed that human beings were complex physical machines). Unlike Plato he recommended that a society safe for human beings to live in and prosper should be ruled by an all-powerful sovereign (not necessarily a monarch) whose main task would be to enforce the law.

83. **John Locke (1632–1704):** the first modern defender of empiricism (all our ideas come from sense experience), his great work is *An Essay Concerning Human Understanding*, 1690 (in *An Essay Concerning Human Understanding*,

ed. John W. Yolton (Everyman, 1988)), in which Locke considers ideas, knowledge, language and personal identity. Locke's *Second Essay on Government* is a classic defence of liberalism.

84. **Gottfried Wilhelm Leibniz (1646–1716):** one of the most important modern philosophers, Leibniz defended a form of atomism (nature as we experience it is the result of a vast number of complex atoms which are not physical entities) combined with a religious view of the world according to which everything originated with God's creation. Many of his most important writings are included in *G.W. Leibniz: Philosophical Essays*, ed. Roger Ariew and Daniel Garber (Hackett, 1989).

85. **Immanuel Kant (1724–1804):** one of the most important modern philosophers, Kant attempted to combine what he thought was right about empiricism (knowledge begins from experience) with what, in his view, was right about rationalism (the principle that the most fundamental ideas which structure and give meaning to our experiences are not themselves, as Plato also believed, the result of experience). His most important work is the formidably difficult *Critique of Pure Reason,* ed. and tr. Paul Guyer (Cambridge University Press, 1998).

86. **John Stuart Mill (1806–73):** one of the most important philosophers of the nineteenth century, Mill combined the moral theory known as Utilitarianism (we ought always choose the actions that bring about the greatest happiness in particular circumstances) with a vigorous defence of a liberal political philosophy (there is an important area of life over which the individual should have complete control and should not be interfered with). He also defended equality for women and, rather cautiously, democracy. It is valuable to read Mill in comparison with Plato, whose work Mill knew well: he had read the first four of Plato's dialogues by the age of 12!

87. **Bertrand Russell (1872–1970):** one of the most influential modern philosophers, Russell's greatest achievement was to reveal the logical structure of language and mathematics. It is valuable to compare Russell's theory of the logical structure of language with what Plato attempted to achieve in the *Sophist*, to reveal the formal and conceptual order that made reasoning and communication possible. *The Problems of Philosophy* (Oxford University Press, 1912) is one of his most well-known books.

88. **Ludwig Wittgenstein (1889–1951):** the most famous philosopher of the twentieth century, he wrote two great works, the early *Tractatus Logico-Philosophicus* (in which he follows Plato in claiming that language and the world have the same logical structure) and the later *Philosophical Investigations* (in which Wittgenstein argued that the meanings of words do not derive from 'objects', such as Plato's Forms, but consists in their correct use according to rules). His most important writings are in *The Wittgenstein Reader*, ed. Anthony Kenny (Blackwell, 2006).

89. **John Rawls (1921–2002):** the most important political philosopher of the twentieth century, Rawls revived philosophical interest in the nature of justice, his task being to define justice for a liberal and pluralistic society. It is useful to compare his most famous book *A Theory of Justice* (Oxford, 1971) with Plato's *Republic*.

90. **John McDowell (b. 1942):** one of the most distinguished living philosophers, McDowell recommends that we 'delete' the boundary between mind and world established by Descartes. This does not imply that McDowell defends materialism, the theory that identifies the mind with the body, more precisely with the brain. McDowell also defends a view of meaning that he calls 'naturalized Platonism'. See John McDowell, *Mind and World* (Harvard University Press, 1994).

10 problems in modern philosophy originating from Plato

91. **Mind and body:** Plato distinguished between the soul and the body as two essentially different 'things'; a modern materialist is likely to identify mental phenomena, such as thoughts, intentions and feelings, with physical processes in the brain. Which is right?

92. **Knowledge:** the negative nature of scepticism and relativism, as well as their attractions, greatly troubled Plato. What is knowledge and can it be achieved?

93. **Meaning and truth:** words have meaning and sentences express statements that can be true or false. How exactly should we explain meaning and truth? What is the relationship between language and the world? How do media function?

94. **The real nature of the world:** even though science has been enormously successful in providing us with knowledge of the world, puzzling questions concerning the ultimate nature and meaning of the universe and our place in it continue to be of serious philosophical interest. Is a completely naturalist view of the world, one which combines a materialist view of persons with the belief that science is the only source of real knowledge) completely convincing?

95. **The self and personal identity:** for Plato the soul included what we now call the reality of the self, what it is to be a person with a particular identity, what determines that someone remains the same person, perhaps throughout his or her entire life? These continue to raise important questions: what is it that makes us a person? What determines our particular and continuing identities?

96. **Freedom:** modern philosophers speak of freedom of the will, the freedom to determine our own actions, and

contrast it with determinism, the theory that all our actions have causes and, therefore, we can never act otherwise than we do. Plato saw freedom more as a matter of our capacity to resist causes, such as desire and emotional impulses, and thus to free ourselves from their influence. Can our actions really be free?

97. **Religion:** even though we live in a predominantly secular society, religion has certainly not disappeared, with very many people believing that a god created the world and that morality derives its authority from religious sources. Plato, in his late work, the *Timaeus*, suggested that a god created the world by imposing order on an original chaos. Can the claims of religion be justified? What exactly is the nature of religious belief and practice?

98. **Morality:** Plato based his account of morality on the concept of virtue as a feature of moral character and the expression of that character in a person's behaviour. In modern philosophy morality is understood rather differently, either in terms of happiness and human well-being or as a matter of acting out of duty. Can we learn something from Plato's idea of virtue?

99. **Justice:** philosophical interest in the concept of justice was revived by the publication of John Rawls' book *A Theory of Justice* in 1971 and that of Robert Nozick's *Anarchy, State, Utopia* in 1972. Each author defended his own version of a liberal idea of justice in a democratic society. The principles of justice, a topic initiated by Plato, remains an issue of fundamental importance.

100. **Art:** even though he viewed art with suspicion, Plato understood and evaluated works of art in terms of concepts such as elegance and beauty and emphasized the importance of good taste and judgement. Do such ideas as beauty, elegance and taste have any place in understanding and evaluating contemporary art?

Further reading

Gail Fine, ed. *Plato 1: Metaphysics and Epistemology* (Oxford: Oxford University Press, 1999).

Gail Fine, ed. *Plato 2: Ethics, Politics, Religion and the Soul* (Oxford: Oxford University Press, 1999).

Julius Moravcsik, *Plato and Platonism* (Oxford: Blackwell, 1992).

Gail Fine, *Plato on Knowledge and Forms* (Oxford: Oxford University Press, 1992).

Lloyd P. Gerson, *Knowing Persons: a Study in Plato* (Oxford: Oxford University Press, 2003).

Daniel Russell, *Plato on Pleasure and the Good Life* (Oxford: Oxford University Press, 2005).

Malcolm Schofield, 'Plato on the Economy', in Malcolm Schofield, *Saving the City* (Oxford, Routledge, 1999).

Bernard Williams, 'The Analogy of City and Soul in Plato's *Republic*', in Bernard Williams, *The Sense of the Past* (Princeton, NJ: Princeton University Press, 2006).

Jonathan Lear, 'Inside and Outside the *Republic*', in Jonathan Lear, *Open Minded* (Cambridge, MA: Harvard University Press, 1998).

Alexander Nehemas, 'Plato and the Mass Media', in Alexander Nehemas, *Virtues of Authenticity* (Princeton, NJ: Princeton University Press, 1999).

Index

ALL THAT MATTERS: PLATO

Index

About the author

Ieuan Williams lectured in philosophy for 38 years, first at the University of Edinburgh and then at the University of Swansea, specializing in political and legal philosophy (particularly in relation to economic theory, the nature of language and media, and the work of Plato and Spinoza). He was secretary of the United Kingdom Association for Legal and Social Philosophy for some years and one of the organizers of the World Congress in Social Philosophy: Enlightenment, Rights and Revolution in 1989. His publications include: *Plato: Media Theorist*; *Plato and Education*; *Spinoza and Communication*; *Legal Rights and Privacy in the Information Society*; and *Rationality and Human Nature in Economics and the Law*.

Image credits

Chapter 1 Plato © Nick Pavlakis/Shutterstock.com, Socrates © Stefanel/Shutterstock.com, Greek coins © Marques/Shutterstock.com, FA von Hayek © Hulton Archive/Getty Images; **Chapter 2** Map of Ancient Greece © Antonio Abrignani/Shutterstock.com; **Chapter 3** Agora © Anastasios71/Shutterstock.com; **Chapter 4** Motorola TV advert - image Courtesy of The Advertising Archives; **Chapter 7** Vase showing student at tablet © Photo Scala, Florence/BPK, Bildagentur fuer Kunst, Kultur und Geschichte, Berlin; **Chapter 8** Greek vase © Kamira/Shutterstock.com; **Chapter 9** Tate Modern © godrick/Shutterstock.com.